THE LONELY PLANET
GUIDE TO
EXPERIMENTAL
TRAVEL

Rachael Antony

Joël Henry

Lonely Planet Publications

MELBOURNE · OAKLAND · LONDON

CONTENTS

WHAT IS EXPERIMENTAL TRAVEL?

Experimental Travel evades definition, but it can loosely be described as a playful way of travelling, where the journey's methodology is clear but the destination may be unknown.

Experimental Travel renders all destinations equal – whether the end of your journey is a desert island or a traffic island. It can as easily be done at home or away, and it doesn't require a large bank balance. All that is required is an adventurous spirit...

HOW TO
USE
THIS BOOK

This book contains a series of travel games or 'invitations'. In each experiment you will be provided with a **hypothesis** to explore, suggested **apparatus** or equipment you may need, and a **method** you can follow. In addition, the **introductory notes** provide a little background to the experiment and provide a starting point for your explorations, while a **laboratory report** will enable you to enjoy the adventures of those who have gone before you. In some instances more than one laboratory report has been provided when the experiment lends itself to a number of interpretations. At other times we've also included **tips, variations** and other relevant information. A **difficulty rating** ranks the experiment from one to five (one is easiest, five is most difficult).

In all cases you are free to improvise as you wish. Ideally, this book will inspire some new and wonderful travel experiments of your own. In addition to the travel experiments in this book, which are presented in alphabetical order, you can also create your own journeys by playing with our **Travel Pie: 10,000,000,000 Impossible Journeys** (see p260) or even create your own world with our cut-up **World Map** (see p272). However and wherever you choose to use this book, the only limits to your adventures will be your own imagination.

Tedious legal disclaimer
None of the experiments in this book involve nasty chemicals, but remember that the laboratory is not as confined as usual! If you decide to conduct a travel experiment, use your common sense: you are responsible for your own actions and should exercise proper care for your own safety, the safety and rights of others and the environment. In our lawyers' less than subtle words, 'To the maximum extent permitted, Lonely Planet disclaims all liability arising from the use of this book'.

Q & A WITH
RACHAEL ANTONY
& JOËL HENRY

RACHAEL ANTONY

As the daughter of a pseudo-secret agent, Melbourne-based freelance journalist Rachael Antony began her Experimental Travels in India in 1978 at the age of four. Since then she's travelled the globe for both work and pleasure, and experienced varying degrees of adventure along the way. Having contributed to travel publishers ranging from Lonely Planet to *Wallpaper* Magazine*, she is now working on a low-brow bestseller of the airport variety. Her ambition is to create a Velcro-based art installation entitled *Sticky*.

In addition to undertaking several experiments and providing much of the writing for this book, Rachael also acted as Experimental Travel HQ, liaising with a strange yet wonderful multitude of contributors from around the world.

JOËL HENRY

Journalist and writer Joël Henry was born in Strasbourg, France, in 1955. He has been in turn a photographer, social worker, bookseller, inventor of parlour games and organiser of spontaneous events, including two biennales of edible art and an exhibition of photo-booth art. In 1990, he founded Latourex (Laboratory of Experimental Travel; see p25) with two friends.

For this book Joël shared his Experimental Travel ideas with our intrepid contributors, and retested and reported on his travel exploits of the last 15 years. He also embarked on a diverse range of adventures that saw him, among other things, singing to *The Sound of Music* in Austria, undertaking a romantic quest in Venice and travelling blindfolded to Belgium.

Do you have any advice for travellers wanting to try Experimental Travel for the first time?

Joël: Do it for fun, and for pleasure, but not out of a sense of duty. Personally, I find that having the objective of inventing a new game (as a result of the experiment) is a good idea.

Rachael: Have fun with it, and don't be afraid to experiment further – feel free to play with and bend the rules at any time.

Does Experimental Travel require any particular equipment?

Joël: I don't think so. I suppose you could have a dice, but you can always just toss a coin. I like to take a bicycle (a red, collapsible one).

Rachael: While a gold frequent-flyer account will help with some of the more exotic experiments, the only thing you really need is an open mind. In any case, even the long-distance experiments in this book can be easily adapted to your home town. For once, money is no object.

Do you find the rules of Experimental Travel constricting?

Joël: Experimental Travel is travel with constraints, but at the same time you feel liberated from the limitations and expectations of classic tourism. By travelling with the constraints of Experimental Travel, you conversely have more freedom.

For instance, I once spent an entire weekend playing Monopoly Travel (see p176). Everything was ruled by the game, and no other decisions had to be made. It can be a strange way to spend your time if you're not used to it, but it can be restful. It imposes constraints, but you feel very free; you just have to follow the rules. Constraints help to give a definition to the experience. Another example is A–Z Travel (see p50) – you don't have to think of any other way to explore a city.

Rachael: From my own experience, and having worked with the writers who have contributed to this book, I think the rules create, rather than constrict, the experience. In this sense, I find the rules have a creative and positive impact.

It sounds as though the rules are integral to the experience – but is it okay to cheat?

Joël: I don't believe that cheating kills the game – it's another way of keeping it going. Ultimately, a game is played for pleasure. If you like to cheat, then you must cheat. But it's a question of balance – if you cheat too much, then you can lose the point of the game. If something is improved by cheating, then you must not hesitate to do so.

Rachael: The important thing to remember is that the rules are there to help, guide or enhance the experience. They're not designed to make you have a bad time. Feel free to improvise at any stage!

Is having a guide to Experimental Travel against the spirit of Experimental Travel?

Joël: No, as long it's not a 'bible' but, like this one, just a collection of travel games. Think of them as 'invitations' to be adapted or – even better – completed by each traveller's personal input. A guide to Experimental Travel is by nature a work in progress without end.

Rachael: This book is a guide in the most benign sense of the word; it's really just a starting point for your travels. Following it to the letter and reading it from A to Z is not really what it's about – unless you decide to create a game out of doing so.

How do you think Experimental Travel could develop in the future?

Joël: It's difficult to say. It's a bit like exploring a city according to Alternating Travel (take the first left, then the first right, etc; see p48) or A–Z Travel (see p50) – you never know what you will find in the next street. The search for new experimental ways of travelling is a form of Experimental Travel in itself!

I have a few themes in mind; for example, Artistic Tourism could be based on artistic movements or schools (eg Impressionist, Expressionist, Pre-Raphaelite, Cubist, Surrealist, Abstract, Pop, Minimalist, etc). I'm also interested in the concept of ecological or sustainable tourism, and would like to experiment with games that have a soft impact on the environment.

Rachael: There seems to be an increase in the number of people adapting and applying high-tech gizmos such as GPS devices and mobile phones to existing Experimental Travel concepts, or as a means of developing new ones. Technology is being used in a number of ways, from the fairly practical application of GPS devices by the Degrees Confluence Project (see p96) and using them in an artistic or political way to draw lines on the landscape (see p218) to using a mobile phone to checkmate your partner on a chessboard the size of a city grid (see p156).

Have you had any exciting adventures in the course of your Experimental Travels?

Joël: Yes, many. For instance, my wife, Maïa, and I were recently playing A–Z Travel in Rome. We began in the suburbs, so the majority of our walk took place in parts of Rome that usually hold no interest for tourists. We were passing through the bohemian outskirts of Trastevere on a Friday afternoon when we saw some posters for the opening of an exhibition of Yoko Ono's work. It was a small gallery, with maybe 40 people in it, so we went in. Then we saw cameras flashing and we realised that Yoko Ono was actually there. So I approached her and I tried to explain Latourex to her in 20 seconds and gave her a postcard. She sent it back to Latourex as part of an art project we were doing.

In 1992 a friend of mine found 3000 postcards in a bin. They were all printed with the same image of a Strasbourg hotel. We handed them out to friends and strangers alike, asking them to take the postcards away with them when they went on holidays and to post them back to Latourex. Most of the postcards were sent back bearing drawings and collages. It's a fine collection. (See the following two pages for some examples.)

Rachael: I think Experimental Travel is exciting because your experience of a place changes in line with your expectations. For instance, finding yourself in an industrial wasteland in any other circumstances could be a charmless or even horrible experience. But if you are actively seeking out these places during your travels, you are free to appreciate them for what they are, and you may perhaps even enjoy them. All destinations are rendered equal. This is the most exciting thing for me: to be liberated from the expectations of typical tourism means that the world opens up before you.

What is the most memorable Experimental Travel experience you've had?

Joël: Blind Man's Buff Travel was a very powerful experience (see p76).

Rachael: Even though I didn't end up going anywhere, Taking a Line for a Walk (see p218) was strangely empowering, albeit in a small, personal way.

THE
STRASBOURG
HOTEL
POSTCARD
PROJECT

A POTTED
HISTORY OF
EXPERIMENTAL
TRAVEL

THE HISTORY OF EXPERIMENTAL TRAVEL HAS BEEN DESCRIBED AS 'PLEASINGLY VAGUE'. LESS A MOVEMENT AND MORE A NOTION, EXPERIMENTAL TRAVEL HAS ITS ROOTS IN THE VARIED PRACTICES AND PHILOSOPHIES OF MODERN ALTERNATIVE THINKERS, FROM THE SURREALISTS TO THE PSYCHOGEOGRAPHERS OF MORE RECENT TIMES.

EARLY TRAVELLERS

The concept of travel is not new. Homer's *Odyssey* provided us with an enduring travel myth, and from Adam and Eve's first tentative steps beyond the Garden of Eden to Joseph and Mary's travels on the road to Bethlehem, the Bible is full of tales of travel, adventure, danger, transport difficulties and the perils of trying to find a room in peak season (resulting in the birth of the baby Jesus in a stable). Religions of all kinds have provided the impetus for long-distance pilgrimages: Muslims travel to Mecca, Jews to Israel and Buddhists to India, while Catholics get their spiritual passports stamped in Rome. Many of Europe's greatest churches, such as Canterbury Cathedral (the destination for Chaucer's pilgrims in his bawdy *Canterbury Tales*), were built in order to attract pilgrims and cash in on the pilgrim 'dollar'.

Business travellers have also crisscrossed the continents for centuries, and were particularly busy tying up the Silk Road with peak-hour traffic throughout the Middle Ages. The Age of Exploration, chiefly the 15th and 16th centuries, saw unprecedented parties of would-be heroes set off in all directions from Europe – a trend that would last until the end of the 18th century. And of course, nomadic peoples from the Gypsies of Europe to the Australian Aborigines have wandered the globe for eons – until recently, that is, when colonialism and capitalism divvied the world up into bite-sized pieces and began enforcing border controls. Travels far and near have also been embarked upon in the interests of war.[1] But while trade, profit, religion and invading one's neighbours' lands have always provided a motive for travel, the idea of travelling for fun is a relatively new phenomenon.

---

1. The concept of war as travel is encapsulated by the cult, tongue-in-cheek T-shirt slogan: *Join the Army. Travel to exotic places. Meet interesting people. And kill them.*

WISH YOU WERE HERE...

The first instances of pleasure tourism, and indeed experimental tourism, can be traced to the Grand Tours of the 18th century, when young aristocrats, chiefly male and British, were sent off to Europe on educational missions in search of 'culture'. At the time, the idea of willingly leaving home in order to travel abroad for pleasure was highly original and more than a little experimental. The Grand Tourists' destinations of choice were the highly exotic Italy, namely Florence and Venice, and also parts of France and Spain. Accompanied (if not closely supervised) by their tutors, it was hoped that these fine young men would, in the course of their travels, acquire superior language and diplomatic skills, develop good manners

TOURIST

The precise origins of the word 'tourist' are unclear. According to the French dictionary *Le Petit Robert*, the word was first coined in 1811 and introduced to France by Stendhal, who used it in 1838 in the title of his bestseller *Les Mémoires d'un Touriste*. More recently, Jean-Didier Urbain, a specialist in the history of travel, revealed that the word was first used by an (unnamed) English writer in 1792. Whatever its origins, the word has certainly proved catchy!

and give up their childish habits. Alas, rather than leaving their bad habits behind, these chaps simply picked up new ones, such as drinking, gambling, wenching and mixing with the wrong crowd. (Anyone who has taken a gap year, booked an under-30s package tour or spent a summer in Ibiza recently will no doubt be familiar with some of these pursuits.)

In 1536 transportation was combined with the pleasure-travel cause when Englishman Richard Hore invited 30 London aristocrats to join him on a highly novel outing: the world's first sightseeing cruise. It ended badly,[2] but started a trend nonetheless.

I THINK, THEREFORE I TRAVEL

The continuing popularity of leisurely travel experiments was inspired by the exploits of explorers such as Captain James Cook (1728–79), who headed off to the South Seas in the interests of colonialism, and Charles Darwin (1809–82), who, in the name of science, embarked on the most ambitious souvenir-collecting tour in the history of humankind. The journeys of this era reflected the popular notions of the Age of Enlightenment, which sought to impose a rational and scientifically proven order onto what was seen as the earth's natural chaos. The

---

2. During their journey to the New World they became stranded off the coast of Newfoundland. Finding themselves with insufficient provisions, they ended up eating each other. It's worth noting that the 'new world' was old news to the people who lived there.

concepts of widening one's intellectual horizons through science and widening the West's horizons – both cultural and physical – via colonialism dovetailed with the notion that individuals might widen their own lives by seeking out new experiences via travel.

Other key figures of the time included Sir Isaac Newton, creator of physics; the Prussian philosopher Immanuel Kant (also a key influence on the Romantics), who coined the motto: 'Have courage to use your own intelligence!'; and Diderot and the French Encyclopedists. The breakdown of old belief systems was mirrored in the shaking off of old power structures, with revolutions in both America (1775–83) and France (1789–99). It was also at this time that the metric system was invented, and increasingly precise mapping of the world took place, made necessary by the European 'discovery' and division of the world into imperial territories.

If travel during the Age of Enlightenment was a means of discovery and research, for the Romantics, who arose partially in opposition to this rational era, travel was more likely to be seen as a means of spiritual discovery and, as advocated by the philosopher Jean-Jacques Rousseau, a way of returning to nature. The Romantic poets William Wordsworth and Samuel Taylor Coleridge were among those who took long, reflective strolls and climbed mountains in the name of travel, and of art.[3] Wordsworth's poetry is now synonymous with the landscape of the English Lake District. The opium-eating writer Thomas de Quincey, their contemporary, was a walker too, but of London's shady nether world – a pursuit that has more in common with the seemingly aimless drifting later championed by the Situationists (see p21). Alongside these artists who incorporated their travels into art, and vice versa, were upper- and middle-class travellers such as those who experimented with taking the thermal waters in Bath.

The Industrial Revolution brought wads of cash to England's rising upper classes. Rolling in dough but short on sophistication, the nouveaux riches took to Europe in their droves – their Baedeker or Murray travel guides in hand – grimly determined to acquire culture and personal betterment, or at the very least give the appearance of doing so.

ORGANISED FUN

In 1841 Thomas Cook organised the world's first rail package tour for 500 temperance campaigners, taking them from Leicester to Loughborough – all of 20 miles away. Complete with organised games, tea and a brass band, the expedition was such a success that Cook was inspired to make tourism his business. Thirty years later he organised his first round-the-world tour (in 222 days).

---

3. According to the critic Robin Jarvis, Coleridge ceased to write blank verse after he stopped his habitual long walks. See Rebecca Solnit, *Wanderlust: A History of Walking* (London: Verso, 2001).

GUIDES FOR TRAVELLERS

The first known travel guide was *A Guide for Travellers on the Continent* by Mariana Starke, published in 1820 by John Murray, who was also the publisher of Lord Byron's poetry. Starke's guide formed the model for both the Baedeker and Murray guides that followed. The classic Baedeker travel guides, published from 1832 to 1943, were the first to use ranking devices such as asterisks to 'rate' sights and attractions, and were packed with tips on transport, accommodation and cultural insights:

> [Englishmen] have a reputation for pugnacity in France; let them therefore be especially cautious not to make use of their fists, however grave the provocation, otherwise they will rue it. No French magistrate or judge will listen to any plea of provocation; fine and imprisonment are the offender's inevitable portion.[4]

Other guides catered for an emerging niche market. May Alcott Nieriker (sister of *Little Women* author Louisa May Alcott), for instance, wrote a guide for women called *Studying Art Abroad, and How to Do It Cheaply* in 1879. Mark Twain's *Innocents Abroad,* an account of his Grand Tour through Europe and the Middle East, became a bestseller, selling 70,000 copies in its first year of publication in 1869.

With the coming of the railway (developed in the 1820s and '30s), the automobile (first conceived in the 18th century but not mass-produced until the early 20th century), the aeroplane (the Wright brothers' first controlled, sustained flight took place in 1903) and the awarding of paid leave for employees (a 20th-century invention), leisure travel really took off. The P&O cruiser and the first-class sleeper carriage became synonymous with glamour and adventure.

Thus travel was conceptualised as a commodity – an experience that one could simply buy – and for the first time, cities, countries and entire continents became something that one could 'do'.

KING OF THE ROAD

The first automobile patent in the United States was granted to Oliver Evans back in 1789 – the same year the French Revolution began. Evan's vehicle was not only the first American automobile, but – indicative of the experimental ingenuity of the time – it was also the world's first amphibious car. Powered by steam, it had wheels to zip along on land and a paddle wheel for use in the water – pre-empting Secret Agent James Bond's fantasy vehicles by almost 200 years.

---

4. Alan Sillitoe, *Leading the Blind: A Century of Guidebook Travel 1815–1914* (London: Papermac, 1996), p4.

LET CHANCE BE YOUR GUIDE

A throw of the dice will never do away with chance.

Stéphane Mallarmé

The world was a less certain place after the horrors of World War I, when the West's faith in scientific rationalism was betrayed by the truths of pure violence. More people than ever before had crisscrossed the globe, as the European powers plundered their colonial populations to bolster their armies, but terribly few had survived the experience. The mood of the time was reflected in the cynicism and deliberate irrationality of movements such as the Nihilists, Dadaists and Surrealists. Influenced by the Symbolist poet Stéphane Mallarmé, the Dadaists founded the concept of anti-art in response to the blood bath of World War I. Key artists of the intermingling Dada and Surrealist groups included Marcel Duchamp,[5] Salvador Dalí, René Magritte, Max Ernst and Man Ray.

According to Hans Richter, Dadaist painter and film maker, Dada thrived on the 'tension between premeditation and spontaneity... The realisation that reason and anti-reason, sense and nonsense, design and chance, consciousness and unconsciousness, belong together as necessary parts of the whole – this was the central message of Dada.'[6] This definition of Dadaist art practices is also a useful means of understanding the philosophies and fundamental principles of Experimental Travel.

In 1921, as just one of a frenzy of other Dadaist activities, a number of artists decided to organise some 'excursions and walks', the esoteric purpose of which was to 'remedy the incompetence of guides...and discover the places that really have no reason to exist'. The first – and only! – of these walks took place in Paris on 14 April 1921, announced by a now-famous Dadaist flyer and attended by 11 people, including André Breton, Louis Aragon, Philippe Soupault, Francis Picabia, Tristan Tzara, Paul Éluard and Georges Ribemont-Dessaignes. Following the publication of the 'automatic' book *Magnetic Fields,*[7] coauthored by André Breton and Philippe Soupault, and the merging of the Dadaists into the Surrealists in 1923, the habit of taking walks through Paris without purpose continued to be an integral part of the group's philosophy, but as an individual rather than a collective event.

For the Surrealists, the focus of interest was not travel per se, but rather the celebration of Paris as a kind of habitat. They explored the secret side of the city, the random encounters made within it and the personal significance of its public places. The Surrealists were at home in the city, and were influenced by the *flâneur* depicted by the poet Charles Baudelaire:

5. Marcel Duchamp is associated with both the Dadaist and Surrealist movements, although he typically claimed to be a member of neither. 6. Hans Richter, *Dada Art and Anti-Art* (London: Thames & Hudson, 1966), pp60, 64. 7. Its original French title is *Les Champs Magnétiques*.

The crowd is his element, as the air is that of birds and water of fishes. His passion and his profession are to become one flesh with the crowd. For the perfect *flâneur*, for the passionate spectator, it is an immense joy to set up house in the heart of the multitude, amid the ebb and flow of movement, in the midst of the fugitive and the infinite. To be away from home and yet to feel oneself everywhere at home; to see the world, to be at the centre of the world, and yet to remain hidden from the world.[8]

Louis Aragon's novel *Paris Peasant*[9] (1926) pre-empted a Psychogeographic (see p23) approach to the city. His book mapped the secret sensual life of Paris, from the chance for fleeting body contact amid the crush of the metro to the unacknowledged eroticism of a visit to the hairdresser's, a class of workers that Aragon urged be educated in the art of the 'geography of pleasure' with 'special atlases', from which 'maps [they] will learn to let their fingers stray across skulls...'.[10]

Breton's novel *Nadja* (1928) experimented with another Surrealist concern: the concept of chance. A fictionalised rendition of his real-life relationship with a young woman, *Nadja* documented and explored the consequences of a chance meeting in the city streets.[11] The Surrealists used the city as a medium, as they did their canvases, and in this way the city walk was as much a part of their work as Dal's melting clocks or Miró's abstract paintings.

The irreverent philosophies of Dada and Surrealism were widely influential. The flavour of their experimentation and their penchant for playing games can be seen in some of the travel games included in this book; for example, their Exquisite Corpse (see p138); their cut-up techniques; their automatic drawing and writing (see p62); and their fascination with chance, word play and combinations (such as Raymond Queneau's *One Hundred Million Million Poems*; see the Travel Pie on p260). While officially 'dead', Surrealism remains fertile ground for any would-be Experimental Traveller.

URBAN AS UTOPIAN

World War II left cities devastated and unprecedented numbers of people homeless. Seeking to embrace a new internationalism that would bring conflicts between states to an end – epitomised by the founding of the United Nations in 1945 – architects including Le Corbusier, Ludwig Mies van der Rohe, Walter

8. Charles Baudelaire, The *Painter of Modern Life*, translated by Jonathan Mayne (London: Phaidon Press, 1968) p9. **9**. Its original French title is *Le Paysan de Paris*. **10**. From Jennifer Mundy, ed., *Surrealism: Desire Unbound* (London: Tate Gallery Publishing, 2001), p94. **11**. The consequences of this encounter for Nadja were to be rather extreme. Her passionate affair with Breton began in 1925 and was conducted with the knowledge of Breton's wife. Breton left Nadja in 1926, and the increasingly unstable woman was driven to despair. She was committed to a mental asylum soon afterwards, where she stayed until her death in 1941.

Gropius and Oscar Niemeyer founded a new international style of architecture. Working with governments, some of these architects sought to house the homeless cheaply, quickly and according to the democratic ideals of the new internationalism – whether the so-called masses liked it or not. As a consequence of their influence, large tracts of cities, such as Paris, were cleared between the 1950s and '70s to make way for the new suburbs of high-rise mass housing.

A SITUATION OCCURS

It was partly as a response to the rapid acceleration of urban environments that the International Situationists (1958–72) were founded. Irreverent, provocative and highly volatile, the journal *Internationale Situationniste* defined 'situationist' as 'having to do with the theory or practical activity of constructing situations', but it immediately debunked the definition by describing 'situationism' as 'a meaningless term…obviously devised by anti-situationists'. An esoteric definition if there ever was one, and well suited to a group known for being obscure.

The Situationists were influenced by the Surrealists, even though Guy Debord, their leader, claimed to despise them. Debord was a charismatic but highly tempered sort who wasn't afraid to speak his mind; he once published a book bound in sandpaper so it would destroy any book it was placed next to.

The Situationists feared that cities were losing their unique character and human dimensions, and that human life was becoming increasingly commodified through urbanism, mass media and the modern structure of working life that divided an individual's personality into polarised opposites of work and play. The Situationists' *dérive* (drift) – an unorganised and aimless yet significant walk – was central to their philosophy of using the city, and was a key influence on the Psychogeographers of today.

The idea of the *dérive*, loosely defined as a technique of 'rapid passage through varied ambiences',[12] sprang from a famous study made by the sociologist Chombart de Lauwe of the comparative mobility of a student living in the wealthy 16th arrondissement of Paris and a worker living in a more populous working-class area. After a year's study it was shown that the student's entire movement for the year could be represented by a triangle that connected her home to her school and her piano teacher's house, with no significant deviations, leading de Lauwe to remark upon the 'narrowness of the real Paris in which each individual lives'.[13]

Members of the Situationists were expelled almost as quickly as they joined, but those who enjoyed the fleeting benefits of membership included the

---

12. Guy Debord, 'Theory of the Dérive', *Internationale Situationniste*, no. 2 (December 1958). **13.** Ibid.

experimental composer Walter Olmo, who comprised 50 per cent of the Italian faction and was later expelled; the Scottish writer/drug dealer Alexander Trocchi, who was associated with the philosophy of the Existentialists and the Beat writers; Ralph Rumney,[14] founder of the London Psychogeographical Association, who was expelled for failing to file a report on Venice on time; the French writer Michèle Bernstein; and the 'Lettrist' Ivan Chtcheglov, who once tried to blow up the Eiffel Tower and was later committed to a mental asylum.

The concept of the urban 'drift' informs Debord's key text, the autobiographical *Panégyriques*, which retraces his perhaps misspent youth with artists, revolutionaries and notable murderers. Other Situationist notions included the proposal by the Danish artist/vandal Asger Jorn that cities be redesigned according to different emotional activity zones – happy, bizarre, tragic, sinister and useful – that residents would 'drift' in and out of. Chtcheglov, who dreamt of the day when everyone would live in their own cathedral, was interested in constructing an emotionally determined architecture, such as 'rooms more conducive to dreams than any drug, and houses where one cannot help but love'.[15] Contemporary architects who claim Situationist affiliations include Bernard Tschumi, who designed the Parc de la Villette (a cultural centre and urban park) on the site of a disused slaughterhouse in Paris.

Perhaps not surprisingly, the Situationists didn't do much in the way of travel – they were way too busy talking, fighting, writing manifestos and being expelled to get much travelling done.

BE REALISTIC – DEMAND THE IMPOSSIBLE!

Guy Debord conceptualised the notion of 'the society of the spectacle', in which real life is replaced with images that represent it. The Situationists have been hailed as the intellectual catalyst for the Paris student uprising of 1968. Graffiti recorded from the revolt reveal a desire for revolution and an ethos later associated with the punk movement of the 1970s. Slogans include the famous 'Beneath the pavement – the beach!', 'Never Work' and 'It is Forbidden to Forbid'. Punk itself became a commodified form of rebellion, packaged by Sex Pistols manager Malcolm McLaren and exploited by record companies and T-shirt manufacturers – an apt illustration of Debord's ideas.

---

14. Rumney later joined the Banalyse (see p23). 15. Ivan Chtcheglov, 'Formulaire pour un urbanism nouveau', *Internationale Situationniste*, no. 1 (June 1958). See Ken Knabb, ed., *Situationist International Anthology* (Berkeley: Bureau of Public Secrets, 2001).

PSYCHOGEOGRAPHY

With the rise of relative affluence in the 1950s and '60s, travel for pleasure became an accepted pastime. The idea of drifting, on the other hand, had been introduced to a scandalised public via the Beat writers, Jack Kerouac's *On the Road* being the most obvious example. In the late 1960s and '70s, travel became an alternative lifestyle choice, a component of the youth and hippie culture package of free love, flared jeans and dope smoking. Thousands of European and American youths 'dropped out' and set out across the globe – in order to find themselves.

Around this time, Fluxus, the offspring of the Surrealist and Dadaist movements, came up with their own games, and turned their attention to the city. The landscape itself became a canvas for sculptors/photographers/walking artists Hamish Fulton and Richard Long.

Situationist traditions such as Psychogeography[16] have recently come to popular notice, thanks in part to the popularity of British writers Iain Sinclair (*Landor's Tower* and *London Orbital*) and Stewart Home (*69 Things to Do with a Dead Princess*). Whereas the Situationists rebelled against urbanisation, contemporary Psychogeographers protest against the blandification of the organic urban landscape by transnational corporations. They also seek to record, celebrate and reclaim the forgotten, neglected and overlooked environments of the city.

Contemporary outfits working along these lines include site-specific art group Wrights & Sites, based in Exeter, UK (see Dog-Leg Travel; p108); the Rome-based group Stalker; the New York-based arts collective Glowlab, founded by Christina Ray; and the French-based group Banalyse, which participated in early experiments by Latourex (see p25). The core difference between these groups and Latourex is that, for the former, travel is incorporated into experimental art, whereas within Latourex travel itself is the focus – any art created is simply a by-product.

OULIPO

The French writing group Oulipo (OUvroir de LIttérature POtentielle) experimented with the notion of writing with constraints, the most telling example of which was Georges Perec's novel *La Disparition* (1969), written without using the letter 'e'. Oulipo's members included the mathematically inclined Perec, Raymond Queneau (expelled from the Surrealists for having an affair with André Breton's sister-in-law), François Le Lionnais, poet Jacques Roubaud and Italo Calvino. Oulipo's influence can be seen in Joël Henry's work with Latourex, in that it is a kind of 'travel with constraints'. Also of interest to Psychogeographers is Perec's 'Places',[17] which reads the city in a personal way when the author revisits 12 places associated with personal memories.

[17]. In *Species of Spaces* (London: Penguin Classics, 1974)

---

16. According to Debord the term 'psychogeography' was coined in 1953 by an 'illiterate Kabyle'; see *Les Lèvres Nues*, no. 6 (1955). In 'Preliminary Problems in Constructing a Situation', an article published in *Internationale Situationniste*, no. 1 (June 1958), Psychogeography is defined as 'the study of specific effects of the geographical environment, consciously organised or not, on the emotions and behaviour of individuals'.

FREQUENT FLYERS

If the social history of the world is ever written, the era in which we live will be called the nomadic period. With the advent of ocean steam navigation and the railway system began a travelling mania which has gradually increased until half of the earth's inhabitants, or at least half of its civilised [sic] portions, are on the move.

So wrote *Putman's Magazine* in 1868,[18] but much the same thing could be written today. Travel in the affluent world has well and truly entered the mainstream. In 2001, for a mere $20 million, Dennis Tito became the world's first space tourist, proving that if money is no object, then the sky really is the limit.

Alongside the development of travel as a commonplace activity is an increasing desire for alternative forms of travel, which in itself is symptomatic of travel's popularity. Experimental Travel opens up a new field of travel outside the more familiar boundaries of classic tourism. Rather than emphasising the final destination, Experimental Travel focuses on the mental journey, the sense of play and the possibility of discovery. All destinations are equal – in fact, the destination is often unknown, and sometimes you don't even know if you've arrived! Anyone can be an Experimental Traveller, regardless of where you might be or the size of your bank balance.

Travellers have explored the world with a myriad of motivations, claiming territories and raising proprietorial flags – even reaching the moon. It doesn't take a lot of imagination to wonder how different things may have been if great explorers such as Marco Polo, Captain Cook, Christopher Columbus, Charles Darwin and even Neil Armstrong had been members of Latourex, and perhaps taken a copy of this guide along with them...

VIRGIN RUNWAY

Despite the reality of the mass travel market, the myth of unexplored territory – the so-called 'virgin' beach waiting to be discovered by the traveller-cum-hero – continues to lure today's travellers. The contradiction between the desire for fresh territory and the reality of globalisation is encapsulated in Alex Garland's *The Beach* (1997), in which a bunch of travellers are so determined to keep their 'undiscovered' island off the coast of Thailand a secret that they start to kill each other. Douglas Copeland summed up the quandary nicely with two definitions that appeared in his iconic work, *Generation X:*

Virgin runway: a travel destination chosen in the hope that no-one else has chosen it.

Expatriate solipsism: arriving in a foreign travel destination one had hoped was undiscovered, only to find many people just like oneself; the peeved refusal to talk to said people because they have ruined one's elitist travel fantasy.

---

18. Sillitoe, op. cit.

LATOUREX:

LE LABORATOIRE

DE TOURISME

EXPERIMENTAL

'Life is a journey so everyone is a tourist'
Friedrich Nietzsche

DEFINITIONS:

Laboratory: *n*, place where things are prepared, elaborated.

Tourism: *n*, travel for pleasure-seeking purposes in a place other than that in which one habitually resides.

Experimental: *adj*, that which is based on scientific experiment.

Latourex: [latureks] *n*, *abbrev* for Laboratoire de Tourisme Experimental; scientific nongovernmental organisation (NGO). Founded in Strasbourg in 1990 and dedicated to the study of those fundamental mechanisms of human activity gathered under the title of 'tourism', with emphasis on the discovery of new ways of seeing other places.

L ATOUREX was born in June 1990 in Strasbourg, during the course of a lunch I was sharing with two friends and accomplices, François Burgard and Michel Hentz.[1] We happened to be on board a barge-cum-restaurant with the fateful name of the *Why Not?*, and were talking about the approaching summer holidays. We were joking about the role of the tourist we were soon going to have to adopt once again, willing victims of the tourism industry's conveyor belt. Devotees of games that we were, we began to imagine amusing variations on the themes typically thrown up by tour operators. Somewhere between the fruit platter and the cheese, we began to sketch out what would become Latourex's founding experiment.

Our initial experiment inverted the idea of the guided tour group by inviting whoever wished to come along on a visit to a foreign town, with the twist that each person would make their journey not as a group, but under their own steam. We chose Zürich, in Switzerland, a city that none of us had previously visited. As part of their mission, participants had to visit the city conscientiously, taking full advantage of whatever touristic, cultural and gastronomic treasures it had to offer. They were also required to make a literary – or even artistic – contribution, consisting of a brief description of their travels written on the back of a postcard, bought from a souvenir stall. There was no requirement to sign up to anything whatsoever, nor was there any group activity of any kind. Each participant was also required to pay their own costs. Latourex, signatory of the invitation, was not to be a travel agency but a new research organisation dedicated to 'furthering science' – an important distinction, as few people can resist lending science a helping hand.

[1]. François Burgard is a journalist and Michel Hentz organises music festivals.

ZÜRICH

We didn't have the slightest idea who would be participating in this stab at synchronised travel in Zürich. As it turned out there were seven of us,[2] and as luck would have it we all bumped into one another at one point or another while pounding the pavement of that austere financial capital, 300km from where we lived. These encounters were handled in various ways: some members of the group decided to hook up and continue their sightseeing together; others contented themselves with a chat or a round of drinks.

On our return to Strasbourg, we gathered like any self-respecting scientific organisation to discuss the results of our experiment. Over a round of vigorously exchanged apéritifs, we swapped our impressions while they were still fresh in our minds. We realised that, over and above the joking, gently mocking spirit that had initially motivated us, we had all undergone a strange and exciting adventure. Our experiment had allowed us to be particularly receptive to the unknown city we were visiting. We discovered that we had apprehended certain things that we might otherwise have ignored had we visited Zürich under more conventional circumstances. Above all, our scrupulous adherence to the preconditions of the journey had paradoxically lent it a sense of unbridled freedom; it was a delicious diversion from our normally humdrum daily lives. We soon concluded that these feelings were due more to the playfulness of our methodology than to Zürich's charms as a tourist attraction. We realised, in other words, that when it comes to Experimental Travel, one place is as worthy as any other.

The first consequence of this conclusion was that it rendered null and void the criteria by which we had habitually chosen our holiday destinations: white sandy beaches, bucolic landscapes or the cultural pull of historic sites. Seen through the prism of the game, a suburb in a small Slovakian centre of industry became potentially as exciting as the Seychelles or Niagara Falls. However, this posed a serious theoretical problem: how to choose one place over another? The choice of destination, after all, is the starting point of all tourist activity.

It became clear that original solutions would be required to define the new goals of our travels. The Zürich adventure had initially been intended to have no end other than itself, but I took the initiative and followed it up by conceiving new projects for further travel experimentation. Thus I became the resident Latourex 'ideologue' – the invention of travels being in itself a form of travelling.

2. The event was held on Saturday and Sunday, 20–21 July 1990.

THE MINI-ENCYCLOPAEDIA OF
EXPERIMENTAL TRAVEL

These projects were collected to form a *Mini-Encyclopaedia of Experimental Travel*. This compendium, under constant revision and added to over the years by several collaborators, has been distributed by mail since 1991 in *Les Cahiers du Latourex*, a home-made but nonetheless richly illustrated publication sent free of charge to several hundred readers who've asked to receive it. Until now there have been 14 editions, several of which were recently made available for perusal on the Internet.[3]

The governing protocols of these travel experiments are multidisciplinary, covering such diverse ground as toponymy, onomastics, pataphysics, art history, political economy, sexology, pubology,[4] mathematics and arithmetic, zoology, aesthetics, meteorology, musicology, numerology, gastronomy, mythology, thalassotherapy, quantum mechanics and poker. They refer as much to the Oulipo movement (see p23), which pioneered writing by arbitrary rules, as to the Dadaists and Surrealists, who had a penchant for marvellous, nonsensical promenades through Paris, and not forgetting the Situationists, who were very active in Strasbourg at the end of the 1960s and whose legacy still reverberates in the city. Their *General Theory on Diversion* was long one of my favourite tomes.

In French, the Latourex experiments are all named according to the rules of scientific vocabulary, having the word 'tourisme' as a base and preceded with a Latin or Ancient Greek prefix. Thus we have Aérotourisme (Airport Tourism; see p42), Contretourisme (Counter Tourism; see p100), Dodécatourisme (Twelve Travel; see p238), Hypotourisme (Budget Tourism; see p80), Similitourisme (travelling to a place that shares its name with a more famous destination, such as Paris, Texas), and so on. In certain other cases, when translation from Ancient Greek or Latin was impossible or gave rise to a monstrous neologism, it was decided to opt for a more banal appellation, as was the case with Auto-Stop Expérimental (Slight-Hitch Travel; see p204).

FROM THE SUBURBS OF STRASBOURG
TO MONOPOLY IN BERLIN

Several of these ideas were subsequently taken up to become real-life experiments. In November 1990, just a few months after the Zürich experiment, about 30 people participated in a 'suburban raid', an attempt at Proxitourisme

3. www.latourex.org. 4. That rich body of scientific knowledge dedicated to the study of pubs, restaurants, bars, cafés, etc.

(Proximity Travel). The experiment consisted of spending a weekend in the suburbs of Strasbourg as a tourist, on the proviso that the downtown area was strictly out of bounds. The data we compared over dinner at the weekend's close confirmed Zürich's promising results.

In 1990 I was a bookseller. I got my hands on an 1891 edition of Baedeker's *The Rhine*, and thus Anachronotourisme (Anachronistic Adventure; see p52) was born. Our visit to Frankfurt followed the itineraries provided in the century-old guide – an uphill battle in a town that was almost entirely destroyed during World War II. The prices of the few remaining hotels from the time had increased steeply, not to mention those of the hackney cabs...

In February 1991, Alphatourisme (Alphabet Travel; see the boxed text A–Z Travel, p50) was tested in Paris by 26 participants who'd gathered from across the country to complete the long march from the Rue de l'Abbaye to the Boulevard de la Zone. Alphatourisme involves travelling from A to Z – that is, from the first entry in the city map's index to the last – by drawing the straightest possible line between the two. This experiment is now one of what we happily call our 'standards' – a method we apply each time we visit a new metropolis.

We devoted New Year's Eve of 1991 to Opustourisme (Opus Touristicus; see p188) – more accurately known as 'new wave tourism' because it takes up the invitation suggested by the title of the legendary film by Alain Resnais and Alain Robbe-Grillet, *Last Year in Marienbad*, worshipped by some cineastes as a masterpiece and by others as the nadir of cinematic history. Thus a Latourex delegation gathered on 31 December 1991 at Marienbad[5] in Czechoslovakia, with the intention of staying until the following year, 1 January 1992. We had the added satisfaction of leaving an altogether different country, as it was that very night that Czechoslovakia was divided into two, to form the Czech Republic and Slovakia. Participants were required to make an artistic contribution in the form of an experimental video or film in the spirit of the original. The results were rather uninspired.

There followed in turn an experiment in Mnémotourisme (Souvenir Travel) in Munich, a series of Rondopictotourisme (360 Degree Travel) garden parties, an Odyssée administrative (Bureaucratic Odyssey; see p86) and a Strasbourg Evacuation to Kehl, a neighbouring German town. This last experiment in Tourisme exodique (Exodus Travel) was conceived as a protest against the staging in Strasbourg in 1997 of a convention of the National Front, France's political party of the extreme right. Of the two latter events, the Latourex activity gathered together the most participants, almost 500 in all. This was soon followed by a Happening touristique (Travel Happening) at Kassel's Documenta, a Nyctalotourisme (Fly by Night – arriving in a place at dusk and leaving by the following dawn; see p144) expedition to Mannheim and an experiment in Monopolytourisme (Monopoly Travel; see p176) in Berlin in 2003.

5. Marianské-Lazné.

Each time, participants were selected by the same means: written invitations were distributed from hand to hand or sent by mail to a network of sympathisers. Information was also disseminated through the media – at first regional, then later national and international – which quickly recognised the scientific importance of the Latourex experiments and committed itself to supporting it. Hundreds of articles and radio and television programmes have been devoted to our work, and, thanks largely to this coverage, we believe around a thousand research volunteers have now taken part.

That said, these collective operations evidently don't exclude the undertaking of Experimental Travel in ones and twos. Thus Maïa, my companion and fellow Latourex traveller from the beginning, and I have tested numerous other hypotheses: Cécitourisme (Blind Man's Buff Travel; see p76), Retourisme (Slow-Return Travel; see p208), Randonnées alternatives (Alternative Trails) and Erotourisme (Ero Tourism; see p120). The latter is an experiment for couples, who arrive separately in an unknown foreign city and have to find one another without having recourse to any means of communication, and without having decided on a meeting place. We have undertaken this experiment six times, and have found one another in each instance. As long-time amateur cyclists, we have also completed a clandestine operation furthering national development by creating and signposting France's first bike path – using several thousand plaques. This circuit of close to a thousand kilometres will henceforth link Strasbourg, the country's most Continental city, to the Mediterranean.

SECRETARIES-GENERAL, ONE AND ALL

Structurally, Latourex mimics travel in its administration. It's a nomadic organisation with no office and only a postal box to receive mail.[6] Its meetings are usually held in a café – each time a different place – and follow an agenda left mostly to chance. There are no legal documents or statutes as such, and all members carry the title 'Secretary-General'.

To become Secretary-General of Latourex, one should have either participated in a Latourex experiment or seriously had the intention of doing so. Failing these two criteria, one simply needs to have the irrepressible desire to become Secretary-General of Latourex.

Joël Henry

6. 3 Rue de Bâle, Strasbourg 67100, France.

EXPERIMENTAL QUIZ

Undecided about which Experimental Travel game might suit you best? Our quiz can help you decide.

QUESTION 1:
Which of the following forms do you most associate with the concept of travel?

1) A straight line
2) A zigzag
3) Parallel lines
4) A labyrinth
5) A circle

SUGGESTED EXPERIMENTS:
1) A–Z Travel
2) Alternating Travel
3) Synchronised Travel
4) Ariadne's Thread
5) Bureaucratic Odyssey

QUESTION 2:
Which of the following numbers or number combinations do you find most appealing?

1) 12
2) 43° 00 00
3) 1, 4, 9, 2
4) 21
5) 1–6

SUGGESTED EXPERIMENTS:
1) 12 Travel
2) Confluence Seeking;
3) Voyage to the End of the Line
4) Trip Poker
5) Chance Travel

QUESTION 3:
Which of the following men would you most like to holiday with?

1) Sigmund Freud
2) Karl Marx
3) Don Quixote
4) Jack Kerouac
5) Paul Klee

SUGGESTED EXPERIMENTS:
1) Automatic Travel
2) All of them except for Monopoly Travel
3) Opus Touristicus
4) Slight-Hitch Travel;
5) Taking a Line for a Walk

QUESTION 4:
Which of the following words best describes your personality?

1) Contrary
2) A Follower
3) Nosy
4) Charismatic
5) Romantic

SUGGESTED EXPERIMENTS:
1) Counter Tourism
2) Ariadne's Thread
3) Travel Pursuit
4) Red Carnation Crusade
5) Ero Tourism

QUESTION 5:
Which of the following animals pleases you the most?

1) Yak
2) Dog
3) Horse
4) Lion
5) Fish

SUGGESTED EXPERIMENTS:
1) Anachronistic Adventure;
2) Dog-Leg Travel
3) Horse-Head Adventure
4) Mascot Travel
5) Thalasso Experimental

EXPERIMENTS
AND
LABORATORY
RESULTS

Aesthetic Travel

HYPOTHESIS: Turn your travels into an aesthetic journey.

APPARATUS: Varies according to your preferred medium, but could include paper and pencil, paints, a portable easel, a camera or a digital recording device.

METHOD: Turn a typical holiday into an aesthetic journey by creating an artistic record of your trip in a systematic but novel way. For instance, in every new town you visit, photograph the fire station or a letter box; write a poem in every main square; draw, paint or photograph the view from your hotel window, the contents of the minibar or what you have for breakfast. If you are musically inclined, consider composing or recording a musical piece incorporating the typical sounds that surround you.

01

INTRODUCTORY NOTES:

There's nothing like travelling to get the creative juices flowing. This experiment gives you a focus for those artistic impulses, as well as an underlying purpose for your journey. It also encourages you to document your travels in unusual and refreshing ways. As a traveller, one expects to see major differences in each new location, but sometimes it's the small things that reveal the most interesting contrasts.

LABORATORY RESULTS

Courtesy of Experimental Tourist
Manu Guillaud, Paris–Tokyo.

Train compartment

Time: 18:00

Subtext: I unload my moving library onto the *Moscow Express*: one-third Japanese mythology, one-third Nietzsche and one-third blank pages for my own thoughts.

There are so many distractions around us in our everyday life that we seldom have the time to carry on any activity for more than a few minutes without being interrupted. I've spent so many years longing for the moment I could indulge myself and do nothing whatsoever but read a huge history book, or Nietzsche, or write lines of Japanese hiragana script. And so I decided to take on the Aesthetic Travel experiment and purposely trap myself in a small room with just a few books – no phone, no watch, no friends. My only distraction would be to bring along a camera with which to take a random number of photographs every day at a random time – from the same window.

I first thought about spending some time locked in my cellar, but there are no windows – and that would hardly qualify as travelling, I presume. It so happened that I had to travel from Paris to Tokyo, so I hopped onto a series of trains – *Moscow Express*, Trans-Siberian Railway etc – which for a few weeks became an idyllic moving jail, progressing across countries as slowly as I was getting through my reading material. Taking a trip to nothingness, I soon forgot not only about daily life but also about my habits, and the rules I usually set myself.

Train tracks

Time: 12:21

Reading:
N. Bouvier, Book 2 / p237

Subtext: A transport hub lost in Siberia. 'We forbid ourselves any kind of luxury – except one – slowness.' (N. Bouvier)

Mountains from window

Time: 06:51

Reading:
Nietzsche, Book 1 / p114

Subtext: Dazed and confused, jolted from my dreams by an early train stop, I absorb tea by the glass. The train is absolutely quiet.

Fan

Time: 00:23

Reading:
Y. Mishima, Book 6 / p159

Subtext: Inside, a fan whirs: staring out at the night I see lost train stations, endless parallel lines of trees, barely lit by the passing locomotive.

Desert plain and clouds

Time: 11:23

Reading:
Nietzsche, Book 1 / back to p61

Subtext: Later in the Mongolian desert. Everything is flat, but nothing is straight. The more the train advances, the further I slide back into my book.

For most of my trip the train compartment was completely empty, and I saw no-one but the Chinese caretaker. With absolutely nothing to do, I found myself placed in a mood of confusion – but it was a sweet kind of confusion. I found myself focusing on little things, such as how best to make a hot drink with the little bags of tea I'd brought along with me. The more time I spent away from my everyday life, the more freedom I had to think. Making the Chinese caretaker smile for once was a highlight.

Desert plain

Time: 4:47

Listening:
Madonna / Track 6

Subtext: Even in Mongolia one can still find signs of *American Life*.

Train seats

Time: 00:23

Subtext: Late at night at the Chinese border: I can't help but become fascinated by a row of bright-orange chairs, shining like four lonely girls in an immense dance hall.

AIRPORT TOURISM

HYPOTHESIS: Spend 24 hours in an airport without getting on a plane.

APPARATUS: Transport to the airport of your choice, money, books, nutritious snacks. (No passport required.)

METHOD: Enjoy the comfortable airport lounges, the different washing facilities, the shops and the various eateries. Watch people skip through to the departure lounge and let your eyes glaze over as you peruse the ever-changing departures board.

INTRODUCTORY NOTES:

This experiment offers the opportunity to turn a place of transit into the actual destination. Airports such as London Heathrow, Charles de Gaulle in Paris and Sahar in Mumbai regularly appear on lists of the world's worst air terminals, and thus may offer an 'extreme' form of Airport Tourism. In contrast, airports such as those in Hong Kong and Singapore are usually rated among the world's best, and are well suited to beginners. Singapore, for instance, offers discovery tours, in-house game shows and a swimming pool.

The airport is typically a place of transit; it's a place that we can't wait to leave, whether we want our journey to begin or not. Most travellers have a 'stranded at the airport' disaster story, though few would compare with the sad experience of Merhan Karimi Nasseri, originally of Iran, who has been stranded at Charles de Gaulle airport since 1988.[1]

1. The details of Mr Nasseri's life are rather unclear. Believed to be from Iran and educated in England, Mr Nasseri was apparently expelled from Iran after protesting against the shah in the 1970s. He was then said to have been refused asylum in England and Belgium, and was arrested at Paris' Charles de Gaulle airport in 1988 because of his lack of papers. Nasseri declared himself stateless and has remained at the airport ever since. He was finally granted a temporary residency permit and refugee passport by the French government in 1999, but the experience has destroyed Nasseri's mental wellbeing and he has refused to sign the necessary documents and leave Charles de Gaulle. The story of Mr Nasseri's life was later fictionalised in Steven Spielberg's *Terminal*, starring Tom Hanks, who has a glamorous air hostess, Catherine Zeta Jones, to keep him company. Mr Nasseri has received around $300,000 plus royalties from Spielberg s Dreamworks film production company, but he is yet to spend it.

LABORATORY RESULTS

Courtesy of Experimental
Tourist Michael Clerizo,
London, UK.

∽✺∽

7.00AM

Want to make your friends laugh? Tell them you're spending 24 hours at an airport. Want to make your friends jealous? Tell them you're spending time away from workaday cares and responsibilities, exploring places, observing people and indulging your inner child. In other words, tell them about the 24 hours you spent at an airport.

Epiphanies are difficult to define and their occurrence is always unpredictable. I'm not sure I've ever experienced one. But trundling along on the Piccadilly Line towards Heathrow airport, the site of my 24-hour visit, a sense of liberation washed over me.

Unlike my previous journeys to airports, I had not once glanced anxiously at my watch. Time didn't matter. Nor had I constantly performed my usual nervous ritual of fumbling through my pockets, making sure I had my passport, ticket and credit cards. All that was for people who were actually going somewhere. Me, I was just going to hang out. I didn't even have my passport with me – just a toothbrush, toothpaste, lots of stuff to read, a notebook and several pens.

I arrive at Terminal 4 and head for the airport information desk to pick up a few basic facts. I learn that the first flights land at around 5am and the last arrive at 11pm. The airport itself and some of the shops in the check-in and arrivals areas never close, but the trains that run between Terminal 4 and Terminals 1, 2 and 3 stop at 11.45pm. A helpful staff member advises me to spend the night in Terminals 1, 2 or 3 because they are bigger and livelier than Terminal 4 after hours.

As Douglas Adams observed in *The Long Dark Tea-Time of the Soul*, 'It can hardly be a coincidence that no language on earth has ever produced the expression, "As pretty as an airport" '.[2]

My plan is to pass some of my 24 hours searching for something 'pretty'. The information desk staff recommend I visit the chapel.

2. Douglas Adams, *The Long Dark Tea-Time of the Soul* (New York: Simon & Schuster, 1989).

'IT CAN HARDLY BE A COINCIDENCE THAT NO
LANGUAGE ON EARTH HAS EVER PRODUCED THE EXPRESSION,
"AS PRETTY AS AN AIRPORT."

8.00AM

St George's chapel is located in the basement of the control tower and looks more like a crypt than a chapel. There are three altars. Embroidered onto the cloth covering the largest altar are three aeroplanes. Inside each aeroplane is an embroidered cross, the upright in the fuselage and the cross-bar extending into the wings. It's a welcoming and peaceful place but more solemn than pretty.

My personal vote for the prettiest site at Heathrow is the entry/exit ramp that wraps around Short Stay Car Park 1. Built from concrete and bricks, the sweeping curve of the ramp is as pretty as any French chateau staircase.

During my hunt I discover some other interesting features: bureaux de change are always situated next to arrivals areas, and the multifaith prayer room in Terminal 3 is just opposite the dry-cleaners.

12.30PM

Heathrow is a big, rambling place, and finding the ramp took four hours. It's time for lunch. Lunch is followed by a long stint of reading...

4.00PM

I'm wandering around again when I have my second epiphany. 'What an idiot I am!' (I'm sure the best epiphanies always begin with that thought.) An airport is a superb place for watching the world come and go. After all, that's exactly what the world is doing at an airport. Except for me – I'm staying put for 24 hours.

I survey all four terminals and conclude that check-in areas are crowded, noisy and full of stress. Arrivals areas are mellower. Terminal 2 has a few rows of comfortable seats overlooking its arrival area. I sit and observe as people embrace, kiss, cry or yell down their mobile phones: 'I'm here, stupid – where are you?'

8.00PM

Hanging around at Heathrow is like staying home from school and spending the entire day in your pyjamas lying on the couch, watching TV and eating ice cream. (I can't think why it isn't more popular!)

12.15AM

At a little after midnight, the show ends. As the food shops close, I stock up on provisions for the night. Inside a display case, I see an example of East meeting West – the last doughnut is sitting next to an onion bhaji. I haggle and get the doughnut at half-price.

2.00AM

I feel sleepy. Hoping for an invigorating sugar rush, I eat the donut. It tastes of onion bhaji. Still sleepy, I decide to try some physical exercise: namely pushing a baggage trolley through the tunnels that connect Terminals 1, 2 and 3. Each tunnel has two moving walkways separated by an expanse of polished marble tiles.

While navigating the trolley on the tiles, the child in me takes over. Holding onto the trolley, I break into a run. I realise that I am reliving a game I played years ago in shopping-mall parking lots. I haven't lost my touch either, because I am still able to judge the best moment to jump onto the back of the trolley and coast to a gentle stop.

2.45AM

Like all kids having fun, I attract the attention of others. A honeymooning couple from Texas, Brad and Amy, who have missed a connecting flight to Italy, have a few goes. Eventually three guys from India join us. We play until two cleaners appear and we have to stop. I suggest that we move to another tunnel and try some floor skating. To floor skate, you remove your shoes, run a few yards in your socks and then break into a slide. Amy turns out to be a floor-skating virtuoso; she can even slide backwards.

4.15AM

We repair to one of the open-all-hours coffee shops for a caffeine hit. Brad, Amy, the Indian guys and I chat for a while and then I make my way to the arrivals area in Terminal 3 to watch the people on the first flight from Hong Kong come in.

7.00AM

Back on the Piccadilly Line, I experience the perfect ending to my 24-hour experiment. I fall asleep.

ALTERNATING

HYPOTHESIS: Discover your own or a foreign town by following alternating travel directions.

APPARATUS: The ability to tell your left from your right.

METHOD: Leave your home on foot. Take the first road on the right, then the next on the left, then the next on the right, then the next on the left, and so on. Carry on until something – a no-man's-land, a building or a stretch of water – blocks your path and you can go no further.

TRAVEL

INTRODUCTORY NOTES:

The brain is divided into two sections: the right and the left. The right side of the brain is primarily concerned with the emotions and recognition of shapes and topographical forms; the left is devoted to logical, communicative skills such as writing (if you are right-handed) and language and numerical comprehension. The two distinct areas (concentrated around the cerebral cortex) are joined by the corpus callosum.

If you ever find yourself weighing the pros and cons of a particularly difficult decision, and find you must choose between two quite opposing viewpoints, that's because you *are*. According to some neurological theorists, each decision requires the brain to take a kind of straw poll between the two sides, both of which offer different, sometimes incompatible, opinions. If someone suffers a brain injury that damages the corpus callosum and separates the two sides, and that person is still living and coherent,[1] you can potentially trick that person's brain into allowing you to converse with its two distinct sides – or 'personalities'.[2]

Using both right and left sides of the brain in equal measures, Alternating Travel restores equilibrium to the decision-making process. There's no right or wrong when experimenting with Alternating Travel: just right or left. The game is extremely easy to play, as you don't have to decide what route to take. It's also exciting, as you never know when your trip will end, until it does.

1. Yes, it is possible!

2. From Richard L Gregory, ed, *The Oxford Companion to the Mind* (Oxford: Oxford University Press, 1987)

Oxford, the city of dreaming spires and the academic elite, is a very divided city with virtually no interaction between town and gown. Clustered within the suburban sprawl is a series of very disadvantaged areas, all with attendant social problems. I live in one of those strange places where a single road divides two very different communities – one side has nice houses, cars and lots of extensions going up; on the other side there's a run-down council estate.

'I'm cruising the estate, walking confidently, with no idea where I'm going but knowing exactly how to get there.'

Right: It's the evening of a Bank Holiday Monday. Petals from a cherry blossom fall through the air like slow snowflakes and carpet the ground in white. The idyllic scene is shattered when I take my first right and see two learner drivers about to collide. One concentrates on a three-point turn while the other reverses around the corner. Each is oblivious to the other. I'm deep in the heart of suburbia; pigeons coo and my keys clink in my pocket with every step. Two men chat over a garden wall, one giant belly hidden from the other by a concrete garden wall. I pass a boarded-up pub but it's the four red wine gums leaking from a wet packet just inside the metal fencing that catch my attention.

Left: Around the next corner a granny is dropped off after a lazy lunch. Her son waves goodbye and she waddles into her house, her lurid orange sunglasses matching the wholly unnatural colour of her hair. Her undyed roots are muddy grey and remind me of the two-tone beard and locks of 'Fat Pat', my old English teacher. Another learner driver does the slowest three-point turn imaginable. There's oceans of room on either side but he's going nowhere.

A–Z TRAVEL

Another way of navigating the city using similarly arbitrary directions is A–Z Travel. Simply open a local map or atlas, find the first road beginning with A and the last beginning with Z, and draw a line between the two. Walk the length of this line and discover the city alphabetically.

Right: I turn into a graffiti-clad laneway and emerge on the main road. The grass verge is freshly cut, its smell heavy with memories that suddenly flood and fade from my mind. The road marks the great divide. I've journeyed from calm suburbia to a run-down council estate in a matter of metres. A child is teasing a Rottweiler in an untended garden strewn with dandelions. I catch a snippet of conversation from behind a high fence and invent a sequence of events leading up to this moment.

Left: I'm cruising the estate, walking confidently, with no idea where I'm going but knowing exactly how to get there. A kid on a scooter flashes past. He has a proper walkie-talkie pinned across his chest – slightly more advanced than the paper cup and string version I remember.

Right: Three girls are skipping on the road to the left, but I'm on course for a right, just past the two teenage girls trying hard not to conform but dressed almost identically.

Left: A laneway takes me alongside the city ring road, cars sweeping by behind the trees. The roads twist and turn and I have no way of predicting where I might end up. At the nearby river? Endlessly strolling down the motorway?

Right: The first right turns me away from the traffic and into another quiet but run-down residential street. My mind jumps ahead to where I might end up and then suddenly I'm there. The first left leaves me flanked by rows of garages on either side, boarded up and lonely. Potholes litter the tarmac, and a massive pink armchair lords it over the scene, weathered by rain and wind and covered in old tyres.

....

MENTAL ALTERNATING TRAVEL

....

Counting sheep is old hat. Instead, Joël Henry recommends Mental Alternating Travel as a good cure for insomnia. Simply imagine yourself doing Alternating Travel in a place you know well until you get lost, or fall asleep. Try not to get obsessed though; getting up in the middle of the night to double-check a location is defeating the purpose.

Like most people, I tend to take the same route to and from work or the shops, and I've never had any reason to go into the estate or any inclination to wander down abandoned laneways. This experiment made me realise how easy it is to avoid whole chunks of your immediate surroundings. I didn't know if it would take me five minutes or five hours to reach my destination, and I was continually trying to guess and reassess where it was that I was going – funnily enough, I was always wrong...

Anachronistic Adventure

HYPOTHESIS: Step back in time and experience travel from another era.

APPARATUS: You will need to acquire the use of an outmoded form of trans-portation.

Note: while this form of travel may inspire the wearing of period costume, it is strictly optional.

METHOD: Travel by an outdated or obsolete form of transport. Suggestions include a hackney carriage, penny-farthing, galley, sedan chair or hot-air balloon.

INTRODUCTORY NOTES:

Travellers undertaking an Anachronistic Adventure can experience the pace and style of travel of a bygone age with greater authenticity than most historical reality–TV programmes, and without the inconvenience of having to invent a time machine. Participants would be wise to note that some forms of transport will involve greater planning and pose more difficulties than others. For instance, those who choose to travel by penny-farthing or unicycle will undoubtedly need to apply themselves to some preliminary practice. (Note: the acquisition of bicycle trouser clips is strongly urged and helmets are recommended.) Sedan chairs are notoriously difficult to come by, and bearers may take some time to 'break in'. (Choose your bearers carefully – uniformity of height will ensure a more even journey.)

The joys and tribulations of Anachronistic Tourism are nicely evoked in Gustav Temple and Vic Darkwood's 'travel memoir' *Around the World in Eighty Martinis*. This comic tome documents how the two 'chaps' take on a wager to travel the globe, crossing all five continents and using a different form of transport for every stage of the journey. Having travelled by yak, balloon and hovercraft (wherein they overcome space and storage difficulties by strapping their trusty butler to the roof racks), they indulge in the rare pleasure of crossing the Congo in a gold-trimmed sedan chair, borne by 'four men in training for the forthcoming Commonwealth Games'. Alas, their passage is brought to a standstill when the pair are kidnapped by gorillas.

I came late to the world of penny-farthing cycling. More than a century late, in fact. When everyone else was discovering bicycles with 24 speeds, suspension and lightweight alloy frames, I was revelling in the old-fashioned delights of the high-wheel bicycle. One speed, no brakes, and a solid rubber tyre on a 50-inch wheel (the world of the penny-farthing is yet to recognise metric measurements). My new steed was a beautiful bicycle, made to resemble an original penny-farthing – handles carved from pale jacaranda wood and the gracefully curving backbone nickel plated to give it a soft silver shine.

I cobbled together a costume to match: a tight-fitting purple jacket with leg-of-mutton sleeves, a pin-tucked white blouse, an original Victorian black ladies' bow tie, a straw boater, a pair of black leather gloves, and a cinched leather belt. I broke with the tradition that saw ladies cycling in voluminous skirts – though no 'lady' would have been seen dead on a penny-farthing in the 1870s, when the bicycles were developed – and adorned myself in close-fitting purple bloomers. A pair of lace stockings worn with high-heeled ankle boots completed the outfit.

And so, suitably togged up in full Victorian costume, my husband, Peter, and I set off through the back-streets high atop our penny-farthings to meet some friends for coffee...

We are in Melbourne, where the graceful gardens and tree-lined streets lend themselves perfectly to such period re-creations. From South Yarra we ride through the falling leaves of Fawkner Park, past the playground where small children stand open-mouthed, strolling couples smile and dog walkers call their charges close.

Onto the main road we pedal, enjoying the quiet streets of an early Sunday morning. On the gentle descent of Domain Rd we pick up speed and fly towards the traffic lights at busy St Kilda Rd. Peter pedals furiously ahead of me, darting across the intersection just before the lights change to red. Flash! A red-light camera snaps my picture. What will they make of that in Traffic HQ?

Both safely across St Kilda Rd, we glide down the peaceful side streets of South Melbourne. Ivy trails over high brick fences that protect residents from the gaze of passers-by – except those passers-by who are mounted 6ft above the ground on a penny-farthing. A look of bewilderment replaces passion on the faces of the couple we spot in flagrante delicto in their backyard.

We reach South Melbourne Market, and compose our faces into casual expressions as we ride past the cafés. Families turn to point and stare, trendy young things pretend to ignore us and middle-aged men laugh at their cleverness in asking the very predictable, 'How's the weather up there?'

Such are the trials of committed Victorian poseurs: the stares, the inane comments, and the blank looks of those who don't want to lower themselves by smiling at the spectacle. We lock our bicycles to a lamppost and sit down to enjoy our coffee. What a way to travel. What a way to arrive.

FUTURE TOURISM

Those who quickly master the art of anachronistic travel may wish to invert the premise and attempt Future Tourism – the art of travelling by forms of high-tech transport either not yet invented or rarely available. Possible modes of travel include flying and amphibious cars, the 'Hummingbird Flying Platform', the 'Solo Trek' personal strap-on helicopter and space tourism.

COMPARATIVE ANACHRONISTIC TOURISM

If costumes and eye-catching modes of transport are not your style, try a more discreet Anachronistic Adventure. Simply purchase an out-of-date guidebook and use it to explore a city, while noting the changes that have occurred over time. Any guidebook will do, though for a classic choice it's hard to go past one of the thousand or so Baedeker Guides that were published during the era of rail and steamboat travel between 1832 and 1943 (available in English, French and German).

• 7

6 •   • 5   • 8

        4 •

                        • 2

        3 •

Ariadne's Thread

• 1

HYPOTHESIS: Let Ariadne lead you through the labyrinth of a new city.

APPARATUS: 'Ariadne', ie a friend, a friend of a friend or an Ariadne chosen at random from a phone directory. Note: it's not necessary that s/he be called 'Ariadne' – Shane, Chuck, Heiko or Marmaduke will do just as well.

METHOD:

1) Find a telephone.

2) Contact 'Ariadne'.

3) Ask for her list of 10 favourite places in the city (or as many as she is wiling to share). Note: these do not have to be sites of tourist interest, but simply places that are meaningful to her.

4) Plot these places on a city map and draw a line between them. This is your Ariadne's Thread.

5) Follow it.

• 9

INTRODUCTORY NOTES:

Summing up the average Greek myth in a paragraph is a little like condensing the intricate histories of a soap opera such as *Neighbours, East Enders* or *The Bold and the Beautiful* in 25 words or less. To summarise, Ariadne is the daughter of Crete's King Minos, the guardian of the labyrinth-dwelling, half-man, half-bull Minotaur. Every nine years, seven unlucky Athenian girls and

• 10 boys are sent to Crete to be sacrificed to this horrible, people-eating beast. Against the wishes of his father, Aegeus, King of Athens, the noble Theseus[1] – who appears to have had a bit of a hero complex – volunteers to be among the sacrificial group, determined to beat the Minotaur and single-handedly bring an end to the bloody business.

Upon seeing the hunky Theseus, Ariadne resolves to give him a helping hand by slipping him a thread, which he fastens to the entrance of the labyrinth. He finds and kills the Minotaur with his bare hands (as you do) and, thanks to Ariadne's thread, emerges to claim victory – and the girl. Alas, the story does not end happily. Owing to an unfortunate storm, or perhaps a god-induced lapse of memory (the reasons are unclear), Theseus abandons poor Ariadne on an island. She is eventually rescued by Dionysus,[2] party guy of wine, women and ecstasy, whom she marries.

Ariadne's Thread can help the modern-day Experimental Traveller navigate their way through the city and avoid the perils of any lurking Minotaurs. Outdoing Theseus on the adventure front could prove challenging, but outshining him in chivalry should be a cinch.

[1]. Theseus, who is raised in ignorance of his noble heritage, discovers his true identity when he is strong enough to lift a large rock under which his father has hidden a sword and a pair of sandals (the ancient Greek equivalent of a credit card and a pair of Birkenstocks). Theseus leaves his mother and sets out for Athens to be reunited with his father, but along the way he experiences a series of dramatic adventures that rival the escapades of Hercules. Travellers who have suffered at the hands of ruthless innkeepers or spent a sleepless night in a lumpy or flea-ridden bed may rejoice in the tale of Theseus' triumph over Procrustes. A truly nasty fellow, Procrustes would offer his bed to travellers for the night, claiming it was the perfect fit for all shapes and sizes. Once the traveller was asleep, he would lop off the traveller's head or legs, or pummel their body with a mallet until they fit the bed. No sooner does Theseus arrive in Athens, where he joyously reunites with his father, than he volunteers for the Minotaur-slaying gig.

[2]. Known to the ancient Romans as Bacchus, God of Wine.

I began my experiment by asking around to see if anybody knew of an Ariadne. A friend of a friend vaguely knew one who lived in Bordeaux and gave me her email address. I didn't know much about her, other than that her last name was Michaux, she was about 30 and she was an agricultural researcher. I sent her an email telling her about the Ariadne's Thread experiment and asked if she'd be kind enough to send me a list of her 10 favourite places in the city.

Her reply was safely in my pocket when I disembarked from Bordeaux' train station on a fine, hot August day.

> Dear Joël Henry,
>
> Having considered your Ariadne's Thread at some length
> – and since it's the first time you're visiting here – I invite
> you to visit the Bordeaux of my first times:
>
> the first time I made love;
> the first time she said she loved me;
> the first time I was paid;
> the first time I drank whisky;
> the first time I sang in public;
> the first time I was in a fight;
> the first time I had my own address;
> the first time I saw a total eclipse of the sun;
> the first time I fainted;
> the first time I saw the Tour de France go by.
>
> In no particular order, these places are:
>
> on the Pont de Pierre;
> 87 Rue Emile Fourcand;
> at the Judaïque Pool;
> at the Bar de la Marine, Rue Fondaudège;
> under the clock at the Place de l'Opéra;
> in front of the fountain at the Jardin Public;
> at the city football stadium;
> in the shadow of the Mission Haut-Brion water tower;
> in the Galerie Bordelaise;
> at the Café Français.
>
> Bon voyage,
>
> Ariadne

And it was a fine voyage, albeit a strange and enigmatic one. Admittedly, I had asked an unknown citizen to plot out on my behalf a circuit through her city as a means of exploring it, but I never imagined she would impinge herself thus on my travels.

Although she was corporeally absent, Ariadne haunted me throughout the course of my journey. Visiting the places in the order she'd suggested, I couldn't help asking myself which particular first time they might have staged. One would expect that it was at the city stadium she first saw the Tour de France. Similarly, 87 Rue Emile Fourcand would probably have been her first address, even if the name Michaux was no longer listed next to any of the doorbells at the entrance. That fisticuffs might have been thrown under the turn-of-the-century cover of the Galerie Bordelaise was within the realms of possibility, and she may well have fainted standing on the diving platform, overlooking the turquoise waters of the Judaïque Pool. But had she been a waitress at the Bar de la Marine or the Café Français? Had she sung her heart out on the Pont de Pierre during one of those annual government-sponsored 'Music Days'? And what had she been up to under that water tower in this wine-lover's paradise, in the midst of these hallowed rows of vines? It would surely stretch the bounds of credibility to suggest that this was the place she'd first tasted whisky…

UNRAVELLING THE SUBCONCIOUS

For the Freud-influenced Surrealists the labyrinth represented the subconscious mind and the sexual and violent urges therein. In 1938, the Surrealist artist André Masson made an automatic drawing (see Automatic Travel, p62) of Ariadne's Thread. Within the drawing is Ariadne – not as a chaste heroine, but in a sexual embrace with Theseus – while a red swirl suggests the violence of the Minotaur's death and the physicality of the human body.

The labyrinth symbol has occurred within varied cultures over the millennia, from Scandinavia and Syria to Australia and Nepal. In medieval times, the labyrinth symbolised the difficult path to God. An example of a modern-day labyrinth is corporate or government bureaucracy, or the Internet.

Dear Joël Henry,

Having considered your Ariadne's Thread at
some length – and since it's the first time you're
visiting here – I invite you to visit the Bordeaux
of my first times:

the first time I made love • the first time she said she loved me • the first time I was

I was in a fight • the first time I had my own address • the first time I saw a total eclipse o

In no particular order,
these places are:

in front of the fountain at the Jardin Public • at the city football stadium • in the shado

on the Pont de Pierre • 87 Rue Emile Fourcand • at the Judaïque Pool

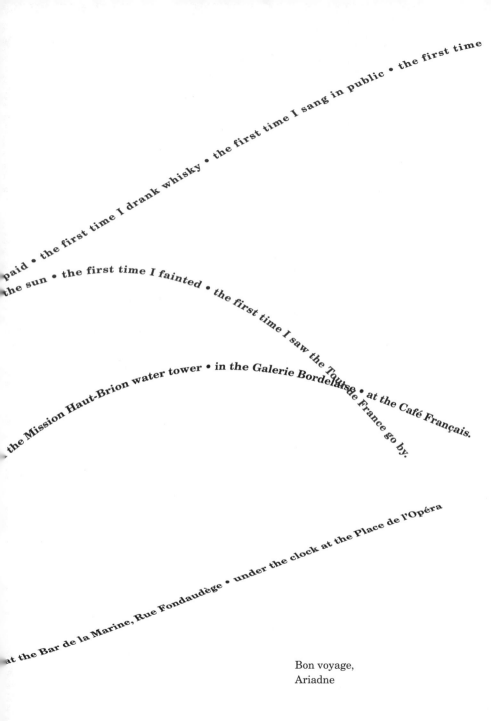

paid • the first time I drank whisky • the first time I sang in public • the first time

the sun • the first time I fainted • the first time I saw the Tour de France go by • at the Café Français.

• the Mission Haut-Brion water tower • in the Galerie Bordelaise

at the Bar de la Marine, Rue Fondaudège • under the clock at the Place de l'Opéra

Bon voyage,
Ariadne

automatic Travel

HYPOTHESIS: Use travel to find yourself: escape from the constraints of reason by travelling automatically (ie without thinking), and see where your subconscious takes you. Apparatus:

APPARATUS: An id,[1] self-awareness and a superego to help you find the way back home. Some training in reaching meditative states could also help.

METHOD: Create a stream of consciousness by following your subconscious urges, free from the censoring voice of reason. Afterwards, look back on your journey – where you went, what you did – and analyse it for psychological insights.

Note: this experiment is ideally practised in an entirely unknown location where you're unable to censor your movements. Ensure that your mind is as free of expectations as possible by not reading guidebooks or relevant literature beforehand. Achieving a meditative state could also be helpful; alternatively, practising this experiment when extremely tired, under the effects of hypnosis or – if you are a sleepwalker – while asleep could also have interesting results.

INTRODUCTORY NOTES:

Sigmund Freud, the founder of psychoanalysis, theorised that individual personalities were formed in part by the interplay between the id, the ego and the superego.[1] His ideas were tremendously influential, not just in the fields of behavioural sciences but in the arts as well. The Surrealists were fascinated by the concept of the unconscious, and they employed various tactics in order to gain access to it. Their methods included automatic drawing and writing, the idea being that via these means one could see the waking world through the dual vision of the conscious and the subconscious minds, usually accessed only through the world of dreams. André Breton's first 'automatic' sentence was: 'There is a man cut in two by the window', which came to him as he was falling asleep one night, an event he later described as being like 'a knock on the windowpane of consciousness'.[2]

Those wishing to undertake Automatic Travel might like to familiarise themselves with Sigmund Freud's *Interpretation of Dreams* (first published in 1899) and delve into his protégé Carl Jung's theories of archetypes and symbols. While psychological insights could prove interesting, it's important to remember what Freud himself once said: sometimes a cigar is just a cigar.

Although this experiment does not appear to be demanding, it could prove to be one of the most difficult to master.

1. The id, the ego and the superego are the three musketeers of human personality, as defined by Sigmund Freud. The id represents primitive urges such as sexual drive and includes the instinctive survival impulses of a newborn child. The ego mediates between the potentially naughty id and the superego, the part of you that has internalised acceptable social standards and norms, and makes you feel bad or guilty when you violate them. Freud advised dream analysis and activities such as free association – similar to that practised by the Surrealists' attempts at automatic art – as the best way of accessing your id.

2. Jennifer Mundy, ed., *Surrealism: Desire Unbound* (London: Tate Gallery Publishing, 2001), p103.

LABORATORY RESULTS

Courtesy of Experimental Tourist Rachael Antony, Melbourne, Australia.

꧁꧂

As a writer, I had toyed with automatic writing, but applying 'automaticism' to travel was another matter. How could I give the self-censoring, school principal of reason the flick and put good old, uninhibited id back in the driving seat of consciousness (sunroof off, elbow out the window)?

As anyone who has tried it may attest, it's not easy to unleash one's subconscious in the hostile environs of middle-class suburbia. I pulled over my car and set it free by the side of the road. ('Run wild!' I cried. 'Don't hold back!') I had half expected it to launch vicious attacks onto passers-by, or at the very least reveal a deeply depraved sexual perversity, but alas there was no response. I started to worry that my poor old id had been well and truly Clark Kented by my 'Super-ego' and wondered if I should relocate to more subconscious-friendly territories (a desert populated by melted clocks, for instance). And it was while pondering this thought that I found myself strolling along aimlessly. I will recount what followed as if it were a dream (psychoanalytic interpretations appear in brackets):

I am walking along a green nature strip. To my right is a graveyard behind a seemingly endless steel post fence (= life journey). I stand on the fence and shout at two gravediggers, 'How do I get in?' (= a death wish?[3] Or simply a black sense of humour?). As I am following their directions, I pass a group of 20 students sitting on the ground cooking on camping stoves (= guilt for neglecting the familial 'home fires'). I am about to enter the graveyard when I see a house for sale that's open for inspection. I cross the road and enter (= desire to return to the womb), and see, in succession: a white coat hanging in the hallway (= a wedding dress); a large print of yellow roses over an

[3] What Freud dubbed 'Thanatos' after the Greek God of Death.

'I stand on the fence and shout at two gravediggers, "How do I get in?"'

empty white bed (= thwarted fertility); a bathroom where the scent of Chance by Chanel still lingers (= risk-taking); wedding photographs over a fireplace (= idealised adult state); and a lounge room where the real estate agent suggests I might 'drink cognac and smoke a *cigar*' (= !). I leave the house, not finding it to my liking (= fear of commitment), and continue to the graveyard (= tendency towards morbidity).

Once inside, I find myself wandering off the path (= dislike of conformity) and onto uneven ground (= life's un-certainty). Angels and soaring crucifixes surround me (= cosmic protection), and in the distance the city skyline juts skywards (= miscellaneous phallic objects representative of men's desire to thwart mortality through the erection of large, man-made objects). The graves are old and falling over (= morbid fear of decay). I arrive at an empty grave without a name (= my own mortality), where I find a broken ceramic wreath of roses (= loss of childhood innocence). I place a circular portion of the broken wreath at the foot of the grave of poor old Thomas Keneally, long dead from Ireland (= make peace with my ancestral past). I walk to the exit (= opportunity), only to find it locked (= my suppressed self), and stare through the steel bars (= imaginary obstacles) at the greener pastures of the park opposite (= penis envy?). I retrace my steps (= look inwards) to reach the commemorative and ever-popular Elvis grave (= father figure), whom I find strangely attractive (= Oedipus complex), and see an 'Exit' sign (= solution). I take my blue suede shoes in that direction and make my way back to my car (= embrace life once again).

Arriving at the car I give a mental wink to my subconscious. 'So,' I say. 'Who's driving?'

BACKPACKING
AT HOME

HYPOTHESIS: Enjoy all the benefits and experiences of a backpacking holiday without leaving home.

APPARATUS: A backpackers hostel, a guidebook and/or map, a backpacking outfit (eg socks and sandals, thermal jacket, beaded necklaces from Bali, a camera).

METHOD: Ask a friend to drop you at the airport. From there, catch the cheapest form of transport back into town, then make your way to a backpacking hostel of your choice and check in. Spend your time eating backpacker meals (pizza, falafel, takeaway curry) and doing backpacker activities with other backpackers – sightseeing, beer drinking, surfing the Net in Internet cafés, having meaningful discussions and even romantic liaisons with fun and attractive people you've just met. Watch your budget, and be sure to take photographs of yourself with your new friends. When you've had enough, make your way back to the airport and ask someone to collect you to take you back home.

INTRODUCTORY NOTES:

This is a great experiment for people who love backpacking, but for one reason or another lack the time to do so. Backpacking at Home gives you the potential to make instant friends with people from around the world, freedom from your usual social routine and obligations, and the opportunity to see your town with fresh eyes, without the disadvantages of sleeping in a dorm for weeks on end and having to lug a backpack around full of dirty clothes. This experiment could be done over a weekend or up to a week – any longer, and you're in danger of becoming a real backpacker.

You could also practise Five-Star Travel or Hip Hotel Travel, but while staying in a swanky hotel in your own city can be a fun and romantic thing to do, it lacks the distinctive subcultural aspect.

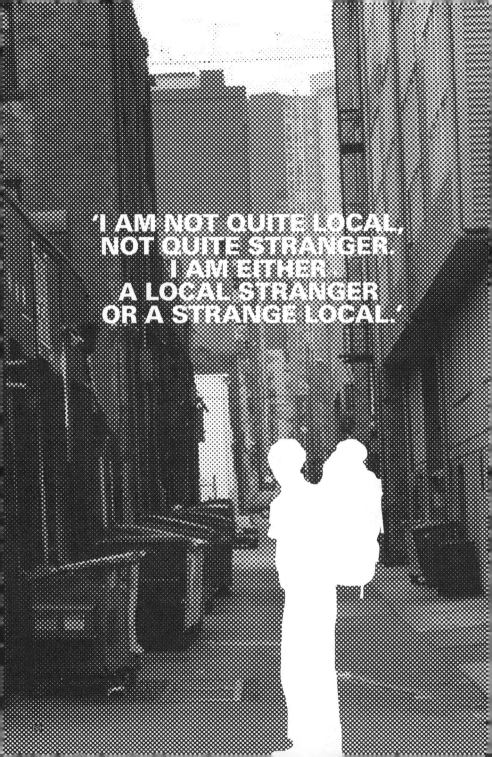

I set off from Melbourne airport on a Saturday morning in a minibus, bound for a backpacker hostel in St Kilda. I've often returned from travels determined to hold on to that delicious sense of freedom that travelling induces, only to be reduced to my usual quivering neurotic state within weeks. By backpacking in my own city, perhaps I'll find out if it's possible to be a traveller in my home town.

The experiment requires a certain amount of mental preparation. A backpacker, after all, operates in a state of near-complete ignorance, whereas as a local I know (or think I know) my city. To compensate, I have decided to pack my bag heavily enough to be unwieldy, and decided that my travels should be circumscribed by a strictly downbeat budget and limited to the scope of my guidebook – which, ironically enough, I have in part authored in my real-life role as a travel writer.

Such a trip from the airport is usually marked by the beginning of a hangover, but even though my head is clear the ride into town is not promising. The suburbs are rendered more humble than usual by a heavy grey sky. Once I've alighted from the bus downtown I head instinctively to the Victoria Market for some lunch. I know a stall that sells the most delicious pizzas and good, strong, aromatic coffee; fortunately, it's listed in my guide. The market is thick with a throng of shoppers, all highly caffeinated and buzzing with nature's bounty. I can usually count on bumping into someone I know at Vic Market and, sure enough, as I'm sitting outside in the cold, turtle-like under my enormous backpack and listening to my favourite busker, my friend H. walks past. I am suddenly aware of the conceptual limitations of the task I have set myself: I am not quite local, not quite stranger. I am either a local stranger or a strange local.

The hostel is described as 'friendly'. This is usually a euphemism for 'cheap and cheerful'. The reception notice board is covered with ads for job vacancies, including one offering $150 for 'nude photographic work'. The lounge area smells of cigarettes and is dominated by a large-screen TV, a pool table, drink and snack dispensers and piles of airport novels. There are signs seemingly everywhere that threaten eviction for the contravention of various rules. The bad weather has kept the backpackers away, and making friends will not be easy. My room is furnished with three rickety tubular bunks, and I'm the sole occupant. The white plywood dresser is decorated with graffiti: 'Remember: life isn't about the destination, it's about the journey', 'Life's short – party naked!' and 'Jesus is coming – look busy!'.

I'd hoped to join the *Neighbours* bus tour and visit some of the sights made famous by the popular TV soapie, but the young man at reception tells me that the tour is booked out (of course, being a backpacker, I haven't booked ahead). I decide to go sightseeing instead. I buy a disposable camera (I forgot to pack my SLR) and, with the camera to my face, I walk into a bench. Two throbbing bruises soon swell up on my shins. Later, at the art gallery in Federation Square, I decide to jump the hour-long queue to a blockbuster exhibition by telling the staff I've left my gloves inside. (Admittedly, as a backpacker one spends hours queuing at train stations, customs points, embassies etc, but as the world's only time-poor backpacker I simply can't wait.) I join the crowds gathering around a temporary bubble-shaped studio where a rock band is recording an album. I lose count of the stunt's corporate sponsors at 37. At a nearby bookstall I buy a book (I buy a book everywhere I go) and run into J., a friend from boarding school I haven't seen in many years.

It rains intermittently throughout the afternoon – it even hails briefly (backpackers don't get to choose the weather). During a squall I sit a Scientology personality test and eavesdrop as others have their results analysed. ('Looks like you're a bit emotionally all over the place at the moment – what's going on with that?') It takes an age for someone to attend to me. I figure L. Ron Hubbard would disapprove of such poor customer service, so I leave, taking the personality test with me as a souvenir. My heart beats fast as I walk away, expecting a Scientological hand to make a citizen's arrest at any moment. I jump on a tram and don't buy a ticket, knowing, unlike other travellers, that the probability of ticket inspectors early on a Saturday evening is close to zero.

I walk St Kilda's streets looking for a place to eat. Thankfully, my guidebook concurs with my choice of the City Cafe, 'a distance away but worth the hike'. But the City Cafe has closed down and is now the Benedykt Cafe. I can only eat in a place recommended by my guide, I remind myself. Moreover, I don't frequent places that replace 'i' and 'c' with 'y' and 'k'. I look up the Galleon, a pseudo-boho favourite, but learn that it's closed on Saturday nights. Next up, the Felafel Kitchen: closed for renovation. International coffee franchise: open for business. I'm reminded that a lot of backpacking time is spent in places where one would rather not be. In fact, time itself seems to change as a backpacker, expanding and contracting like an accordion.

Returning to my lodgings I pass the worst of the many buskers I have seen today: a man beating without rhythm on a toy African drum. Downstairs from the backpackers an English theme pub is showing a football game in the front bar, while in a neighbouring room thin, wispy-haired girls discuss meteorology and consumerism with barrel-chested guys.

Upstairs, life is grim. There's house music playing on the late-night radio and football on the big-screen TV. A bunch of young Brits sip their tepid beers and watch the telly. They must be wondering what brought them here to spend a northern summer in the southern cold, drinking mediocre beer and watching a code of football as obscure as it is incomprehensible. My feeble attempts at conversation meet with disappointing results. A couple of barefoot locals I could swear I've seen before – downtown, maybe

hitting me for loose change – play the Virtual Tennis video arcade game. During cold snaps, when business is thin, backpacker hotels will sometimes offer young homeless people a short-term discount.

After the football game, I retire to my quarters. Tomorrow I will break fast with the young and the restless at the Galleon and visit the biggest collection of kitsch in the southern hemisphere at the St Kilda market. But for now I sleep the sweet sleep of the backpacker. The bunk bed sways to my slightest movement while, downstairs at the English theme pub, the crowd sings along to a covers band – 'Those were the best days of my life'.

....

HOLIDAY MOOD

....

As a variation on this experiment, why not plan a week's holiday within a half-hour drive from home?

BARMAN'S KNOCK

HYPOTHESIS:	Find the area's best drinking spots (and drinks) by following the advice of a local expert.
APPARATUS:	Dutch courage; a map and a friendly face may also be of use.
METHOD:	Go to your favourite pub and order your favourite drink. Ask the barperson where their favourite pub is and what they drink there. Go there and order their recommended drink, and then repeat the exercise with whoever serves you, and so on.
	Note: participants would be well advised not to attempt this experiment on an empty stomach, nor to repeat it ad nauseam.

INTRODUCTORY NOTES:

This experiment gives you an excuse to talk to strangers in the relaxed social setting of a pub or bar.

From Laos to Iceland, the presence of alcohol usually suggests a sociable occasion, whether it's a habitual tipple enjoyed at an Irish pub or French bistro, or the more ritualistic occasion of a birthday, wedding or *kava* ceremony. Officially designated drinking spaces occupy a transitional space between the public and private world, where social norms are relaxed and barriers can be broken down in interesting ways. For example, the fierce hierarchies of Japanese corporate culture are softened by post-work group drinking and karaoke sessions, and the illegal nightclubs that sprang up during the Prohibition era in the USA led to the otherwise segregated worlds of blacks and whites mingling through the mediators of alcohol and jazz. Within Western cultures, the intake of alcohol is also often associated with the recruitment of romantic partners

LABORATORY RESULTS

Courtesy of Experimental Tourist Tom Parkinson, London, UK.

W e started our experiment with a personal favourite – playing table football in our own front room in Clapham, London, drinking super-strength Belgian beer. As there was obviously no barman, Jen, my obliging housemate and fellow traveller, nominated her current hotspot, Dixies, and for the next round a nice cheap bottle of Foster's. We were served by Jonny, possibly Spanish, who directed us (rather unimaginatively, we thought) to the Fine Line chain pub. In the Fine Line we dutifully ordered vodka and Red Bull, and tried to avoid watching the last-ever episode of *Friends* on the big screen. Then, on the advice of our bargirl Bea, we dashed across the road to SO.UK, über-fashionable and ever-so-slightly Arabic-themed, for tequila shots.

We couldn't get James the manager's attention as we nursed a recuperative beer chaser, but we did get chatting to his mate, the manager of another very hip bar, Revolution. Coincidentally, this was exactly where barman Adam dispatched us to next, with orders to try an old-fashioned. This caused our first setback of the evening: Revolution doesn't do old-fashioneds. We ordered bourbon instead, confusing poor Peter so much with our questions that he forgot to charge us. He did, however, direct us to the Falcon, a good old-fashioned (sorry) pub which, in time-honoured British style, closed just as we got there.

Of course we couldn't let one little setback put us off, but it was getting late and the Falcon staff's suggestion of hitting a nightclub didn't appeal. Taking creative licence, we headed for the nearest open bar, the Bierodrome, and sampled some Belgian fruit beer. George kindly recommended a place called Bobbins, but by that stage we'd had enough – bus, pizza and bed took us safely to the end of our journey.

We believe there are few finer ways to discover your area's entertainment highlights than by asking the people who know. We came home with several new friends, a whole clutch of bar recommendations, a dozen photos of confused bar staff and, for some reason, rude words written in marker pen on our knuckles. What more could you want from a night out?

FIRST-AID

To undo the effects of Barman's Knock, a selection of hangover cures from around the world may be of use.

- **Irn-Bru:** a rust-coloured soft drink that smells and tastes a bit like tangerine bubble gum. Guaranteed to strip the enamel off your teeth, it outsells Coca-Cola in its native Scotland.

- **rasol:** Serbians swear that drinking *rasol*, the left-over liquid from sauerkraut, will cure the deadliest headache, even those caused by the vicious liquor *šljivovica*.

- **soup:** a homely cure-all; try the vegetarian-friendly Spanish garlic version or a delicious and nutritious bowl of Turkish tripe soup.

HYPOTHESIS: Explore and experience a new place without seeing it.

APPARATUS: A friend to guide you and a blindfolding mechanism of some kind.

METHOD: Spend 24 hours blindfolded in a new location.

INTRODUCTORY NOTES:

This is an extreme form of Experimental Travel and not recommended for amateurs. Travelling without the benefit of sight will undoubtedly prove difficult, and dealing with other people's attitudes towards you will also be part of the experience. It's important to note that this experiment in no way intends to mock those who are blind or sight impaired. Rather, this experiment analyses what we actually 'see' as a traveller – do we really see things as they are, or are we in some way blindfolded?

Losing a sense can affect people in unpredictable ways. 'The Case of the Colour-blind Painter', recounted by the celebrated neurologist Oliver Sacks,[1] is the case study of an artist who suffered a stroke at the age of 65 and lost not his sight, but his sense of colour. From thereon he inhabited a world made up of shades of grey. Initially, he found it repulsive: the food on his plate was grey, his dog was grey and his wife was grey. He began to refuse coloured foods, eating only black or white substances such as olives or yoghurt. He considered getting a Dalmatian, and avoided making love to his wife. Two years later a possible treatment for his condition was found, but he turned it down. In the interim, he had begun a series of dramatic paintings in black and white. He now shunned the day and embraced the nocturnal world, thanks to newly developed hypersensitive night vision. He even started to travel again – but exclusively at night. He had become accustomed to his new world and now feared the strangeness of seeing in colour.

1. Oliver Sacks, *An Anthropologist on Mars* (New York: Alfred A. Knopf Inc., 1995).

To fully prevent myself from seeing, I fastened one of those oval bandages favoured by ophthalmologists over my eyes, and put on a pair of sunglasses. My wife and collaborator Maïa was to be my guide for this experiment, and it would be with *her* eyes that I would explore a strange city. This was to be a kind of sensory travel, which would test the limits of the visible – something akin to the approach taken by the blind photographer Evgen Bavcar (see the boxed text opposite).

The train taking us to Luxembourg sounded empty, it was so quiet. There was not even a whisper of conversation; only the tinny echoes of distant Walkmans and the occasional ring of a mobile phone. In fact the compartment was packed, but the passengers weren't in the mood for conversation. To the blind man, the mute crowd is undetectable. Halfway into our journey, French customs officers entered the compartment to inspect our luggage. For an instant I wondered how they'd respond if they discovered I wasn't actually blind, but Maïa gave them our passports and everything went off without a hitch.

Once at our destination, we began by visiting the Casino, Luxembourg's museum of modern art. The woman at the register kindly offered me entry at a concession price, and I was admittedly in no state to take advantage of the visual delights on display. Judging from the tone of Maïa's voice, I gathered that the temporary exhibition featuring Peter Friedl – a conceptual artist – wasn't exactly pushing her buttons, but paradoxically the descriptions she improvised were fascinating. As we were leaving I was lucky enough to have several splendid, if fleeting, visual hallucinations.

We went on to wander the streets aimlessly, walking slowly, with hesitant steps. The noise of the traffic all around us was frankly frightening, and I had lost all sense of direction and space. I suffer from vertigo but felt no dizziness as we crossed Adolphe Bridge, which spans the Pétrusse River; by contrast, while traversing the perfectly flat Place d'Armes I had the impression I was climbing a steep hill. As we made our way around the city, Maïa provided detailed descriptions of the buildings and areas we were passing: a monumental sculpture, a teahouse festooned with an Art Deco mosaic, the houses of Place

View of the Adolphe Bridge, and the Pétrusse
River, near the Place d'Armes

Guillaume II, the glass-walled banks, and the sex shops and seedy bars of the neighbourhood surrounding the railway station.

Despite Maïa's patient guidance, all the little gestures of daily life presented a challenge – manoeuvring one's way through a restaurant, sitting down, even drinking from a glass. To simplify matters, we ordered a pizza for dinner. The waiter immediately offered to ask the chef to cut it into small pieces. During those 24 hours of darkness I was treated to no end of consideration. Contrary to what I'd expected, however, blindness hadn't sharpened my other senses, such as taste. Quite the opposite, in fact: not being able to see what I was eating robbed me of all pleasure. That evening in the hotel, having lost all sense of direction and mistakenly believing I was opening the bathroom door, I found myself groping around in the hotel corridor, as naked as a new-born baby.

Blind travel is an extreme kind of tourism, requiring constant alertness. I can't begin to describe how relieved I was the following day when I removed the bandages in the train on our way home. I left Luxembourg having seen nothing of the city, but curiously I've been left with some very precise images. Perhaps one day I'll return to verify just how exactly they correspond to reality.

View of the houses of Place Guillaume II

THE MYSTERY OF THE DARKROOM

The Slovenian photographer Evgen Bavcar has been utterly blind since he was 12, yet his work is exhibited throughout the world. He uses an ordinary camera with an autofocus function, and only sometimes has an assistant. According to Bavcar, 'the visual – that which is seen by the eye – is not the same as the visible – that which is seen by the imagination. Meaning isn't only derived by visual experiences, but also by those that are invisible to the naked eye.'

The 1991 Australian film *Proof*, directed by Jocelyn Moorhouse and starring Hugo Weaving as a blind photographer, was reportedly inspired by Bavcar's story.

BUDGET TOURISM

HYPOTHESIS: Avoid the potential disappointments of travel by deliberately including them in your trip.

APPARATUS: Nothing!

METHOD:

1) Visit a destination that has nothing to recommend it, with not enough time or money and where you don't understand the language. Don't take a guidebook and, if possible, don't take a suitcase.

Or

2) Visit a well-known tourist trap and attempt to survive the experience without spending a dollar.

INTRODUCTORY NOTES:

The two most familiar travel experiences are lacking enough time or money, or ending up stranded in an unpromising location where everything goes wrong and you can't speak the language. The chief benefit of this experiment is that you incorporate all these potential disasters into your trip from the outset, from which point things can surely only get better.

Note: depending on the circumstances this can be an extreme travel experiment, and is not recommended for beginners.

LABORATORY RESULTS 1

Courtesy of Experimental Tourist Joël Henry, Frankfurt, Germany.

The main problem posed by Budget Tourism is subjectively choosing the destination. Where is the ideal spot for bargain-basement attractions, where the locals speak a foreign language? Where's the place I would least like to go on holiday, where the local customs are as hard to understand as the vocabulary? Eureka! I will visit the stock exchange. I'm completely immune to the charms of finance and have always found the daily dramas of the stock market utterly mystifying. The Frankfurt stock exchange is also one of the most unpleasant buildings I can possibly imagine.

This opinion seems to be shared by the young guide in the sky-blue suit who is in charge of showing American tourists around Frankfurt's stock exchange. I've managed to infiltrate their tour group and am amused to hear the guide saying, 'You know, there's not much to see.' It's the first time I've started a guided tour under such inauspicious circumstances.

Our first stop is a small conference room equipped with a video projector showing a virtual tour of this temple to finance, peppered with the cryptic words and expressions we so often hear: DAX, Nasdaq, Nikkei, CAC 40, cash market, stock options... Alas, my English, official language of the stockbrokers' inner sanctum, is not nearly good enough to decipher stock-market code.

That said, it is easy enough to single out the day's cheapest stock, an Italian telecom share priced at €4.36. It's nevertheless way beyond the meagre budget I've allowed myself – one measly euro. In fact, as all transactions must be made through an intermediary such as a banker or broker, I end up keeping this euro in my pocket all day. It turns out that it is absolutely impossible to spend a cent in the place where millions change hands every day. Entrance is free, there is no café, no souvenir shop (no memento pens or postcards) and you can't even throw a tip to the traders from the visitors' gallery, since you're separated from them by a wall of glass. Those wild beasts must be dangerous! Although appearances suggest otherwise, it is feeding time. Sprawled around three workstations, they chomp on spaghetti bolognese from tin containers, one eye on a magazine and the other on TV screens showing the Olympic swimming. They seem oblivious to the columns of numbers carpeting the walls, lending the room the vertiginous feel of a waterfall.

Unlike Wall Street, our guide tells us, stockbrokers here no longer communicate with strange hand gestures and primal screams. Computers have succeeded in taming the golden German boys and girls, even if the spectacle has lost something in the process. Fortunately the visit is not long – over and done with in the space of half an hour. After all, time is money.

'It's the first time I've started a
guided tour under such
inauspicious circumstances.'

**Courtesy of Experimental Tourist Ryan Vickers,
Alberta, Canada.**

I decided to set myself the challenge of spending as long as I could in a tourist trap without spending any money. My choice of tourist trap was obvious: how could I go past West Edmonton Mall, Alberta's number-one tourist attraction?

9.55am:

I arrive shortly before the mall's opening at 10am. I have 11 hours to spend before the mall closes again at 9pm. The first two hours pass easily enough, as there's a lot to explore. My time is spent getting lost, finding two (possible) mall rats and interacting with salespeople. One of my first experiences is with the girl who runs the sweet shop; like me, she is from Atlantic Canada. We have a nice chat, and she takes my picture in front of the giant Pez head.

12pm:

At noon I stop for a (home-made) lunch break. I find that the best benches are located outside the hotel, which is advertising a free audition for *Canadian Idol*. Alas, I'm three days too early.

1pm:

Having eaten, I take half an hour to regain my bearings on Europa Boulevard. I discover the Deep Sea Adventure attraction. Penguin and shark viewings require money, but the dolphin show is free as long as I don't mind standing.

2pm:

The first crisis arises. There are around 800 stores and services in the mall but I can't find a toilet to save my life.

2.03pm:

The situation is averted.

I'm starting to get a bit more adventurous. I chat with a masseur and end up having a refreshing 15-minute free massage on a chair that retails for $6000. This adds to my discovery of free stuff that's available in the mall: postcards, back-scratching treatments and games of video Trivial Pursuit. Unfortunately, the Sigmund Freud action figure isn't free. What a shame.

My halfway point is celebrated in the amusement-park area, enjoying the sight of people screaming on the roller coaster. Only 5½ hours to go...

4.35pm:

I hear a fire bell. This is slightly unnerving. It eventually stops, allowing me to enjoy another home-made snack on the same bench as before.

> **'Unfortunately, the Sigmund Freud action figure isn't free. What a shame.'**

6pm:

Delirium sets in. I have an urge to page famous people over the PA system. I want to go into the casino to gamble. I am starting to recognise certain shoppers. I hear the same song in my head repeatedly. To collect myself, I stand in a sports store and watch a hockey game – nobody seems to mind.

7pm:

With two hours to go, I am starting to think I'm going to make it. I decide to do something I've always thought about doing, and settle into a chair at a bookstore and start reading. The book I choose is about a guy who wants people to accompany him in a movement that has no cause. Maybe I could start one for mall rats?

9pm:

The end finally comes. I toss a lucky penny I found earlier into a fountain. For some reason, I feel sad. I have an emotional attachment to something that is based principally on money. Why?

The mall closes. I open the door to the outside, having survived 11 hours on recycled air.

BUREAUCRATIC
ODYSSEY

HYPOTHESIS: Infiltrate a city and the lives of its inhabitants by navigating its bureaucratic system.

APPARATUS: Red tape; a briefcase and a hurried air of self-importance could also help.

METHOD: Take a tour of places known for their administrative function rather than their tourist interest: waiting rooms, social services offices, town halls, police stations. Avail yourself of the facilities (photocopiers, brochures and magazines, for example) and sample the gastronomic delights on offer (coffee machine, water cooler etc).

INTRODUCTORY NOTES:

This experiment offers a unique opportunity to actively seek out, and embrace, bureaucracy. Given that most administrative centres are under cover and heated, it's an ideal activity for cold and rainy days.

Travellers can prepare themselves for their Bureaucratic Odyssey by reading one of the best-known tales of bureaucracy gone wrong, Franz Kafka's *The Trial*, or by watching the cult comedic British TV series *The Office*. For a Southeast Asian example, look no further than Singaporean Kuo Pao Kun's play,[1] in which a funeral is disrupted when a coffin cannot fit into the standard-sized hole – the message being that in a land where bureaucracy reigns, even the dead are expected to fit in. Ideal locations for a Bureaucratic Odyssey include red-tape heavyweights such as France, India and Vietnam.

1. Kuo Pao Kun, *The Coffin is Too Big for the Hole...and Other Plays* (Singapore: Times Books International, 1990).

LABORATORY RESULTS

Courtesy of Experimental Tourist Joël Henry, S.[2], France.

The Urban Community of S. – the CUS, to the uninitiated – is the city's highest authority. A staff of thousands administers every conceivable residential matter, from revenues to the beautification of roundabouts, the constabulary to the philharmonic orchestra.

You breeze into this concrete Tower of Babel without encountering even a minimal security check. The interior is a virtual labyrinth in 3D. Other than the top storey – level nine, the site of the mayor's office, which is guarded by a touchy receptionist – nobody pays you the slightest attention as you wander through the corridors. It is somewhat more difficult to penetrate into the offices without a good excuse, but in summer the doors are kept open, allowing a summary survey to be undertaken of the manner in which the occupants have staked out their territories. I manage to spot calendars featuring naked women, reproductions of paintings by Miró, a Metallica poster, a superb golden cage containing a couple of budgerigars – and even an assortment of garden gnomes. Enough to make up a fascinating socio-photographic study. Unfortunately, I have only a photo booth at my disposal.

After a thorough examination of the building's various levels, I sink into an armchair in the lobby. With hushed Muzak playing in the background, I spend an hour devouring the assorted free magazines and prospectuses fanned out on a counter. I learn a stack of things – the dangers of natural gas and sex without prophylactics, the approved methods of sorting through household waste and the municipality's successful policy reforms.

Noon's approach brings my mind to thoughts of lunch. In my wanderings through the basement I spot an area marked 'Smokers' Lounge' equipped with a hot-drinks machine that offers, among other things, leek soup. I also spot a junk-food machine filled with chips and chocolate bars. But there's a better option: the canteen. In order to be served, I have to convince the member of staff queuing in front of me to pay for my lunch on his swipe card, in exchange for cash. It costs a mere €3.19 for a delicious salmon and fennel roll, a chocolate mousse and a small pitcher of white wine – to the astonishment of my neighbours, who inform me that alcohol consumption by staff at lunch time is frowned upon. Which is all well and good, but *I* am on holiday, a fact I am unable to hide for long. Instead of tut-tutting, my dining companions go to great lengths to make my stay as pleasant as possible, and list their favourite haunts in the building: a small flowered patio that's favourably disposed to meditative reflection, the gallery of abstract paintings that hangs on the walls of the council chambers, the municipal print room for its casual ambience and intoxicating fumes...

Over coffee I am even able to swing an invitation to an office, that of Mrs H., a bubbly young woman in charge of the roads department. But first I go shopping, for there's even a shop in the CUS. It sells cardigans, windcheaters, watches, pens and so on, all festooned with the town logo. I treat myself to a souvenir travel bag to die for, and several postcards to send to friends.

Mrs H. is reading a newspaper when I enter her office. She patiently explains the long and laborious procedure required to name a new street. As we are getting along well, I go so far as to confess my fantasy of doing her job, voluntarily, for an hour or two, explaining that it would be the zenith of this travel experience. I practically beg her. She considers my request for some time, before concluding, with sincere regret, 'The thing is, there's nothing to do today.'

BUREAUCRATIC TRAVEL LANGUAGE

As anyone who has been 'restructured' knows all too well, bureaucracy comes with its own brand of anti-language, something referred to in George Orwell's *Nineteen Eighty-Four*[3] as 'doublespeak'. Doublespeak is insidious[4], and it can be handy to have a few stock phrases on hand. If travelling to foreign climes, consider having the phrases translated. Note: be aware that your bureaucratic travel plans could be disrupted by industrial action.

2. In keeping with Kafka's themes of paranoia, the letter 'S' is used to disguise the true location of the featured bureaucracy. 3. *Nineteen Eighty-Four*'s Winston Smith loathed the totalitarian society led by Big Brother, and was extremely careful not to reveal his emotions through unguarded speech. This is in contrast to reality-TV's *Big Brother*, which is synonymous with the banal confessions and interactions of attention-seeking people willing to be locked up in a house and filmed 24/7 for 15 minutes of fame and a cash prize. The programme has not been without its critics, of course – especially in France, where protestors ransacked the production offices and attempted to liberate the inhabitants. Meanwhile, the television regulatory body ordered changes to the programme such as 'time-outs' to preserve 'human dignity'. 4. One of the best ways to subvert doublespeak is to use humour. For example, after the fall of the Berlin Wall in 1989, many East German factories were closed, or rather 'wound down'. It became so common that East Germans took to greeting one another with, 'Hi, how are you feeling?', to which the other might reply, 'Oh, not so good. I'm feeling a little "wound down".'

Chance Travel

HYPOTHESIS: Roll the dice and explore the world with chance as your guide.

APPARATUS: A pair of dice.

METHOD: Insert the name of your home town into the index of a world atlas (if it's not there already). Throw the dice, then count that number of lines down from the name of your town. The line that your finger lands on is your destination.

See also Micro Chance Travel (p93) and Coin Flip Travel (p95).

INTRODUCTORY NOTES:

Inspired by an old Persian tale, *The Princes of Serendip*, this is a game for people willing to do anything, and go anywhere. The story, first translated in the West in 1557, gave birth to the word 'serendipity', coined by Horace Walpole in 1754.[1] The Wikipedia online encyclopaedia defines 'serendipity' as 'finding something unexpected and useful while searching for something else entirely', or, as Julius H. Comroe, a biomedical researcher, quipped in 1911: 'Serendipity is like looking for a needle in a haystack and finding the farmer's daughter'.[2]

Serendipitous discoveries include Christopher Columbus' discovery of the Americas (while looking for China) and Alexander Fleming's discovery of penicillin (while tidying his laboratory). Would-be serendipitous travellers may find inspiration in the sci-fi spoof *The Hitchhiker's Guide to the Galaxy*, in which author Douglas Adams proposes that the secret to flying is to throw yourself at the ground and 'miss it'.

1. While searching for a definition of serendipity, Walpole discovered a reference that suggested the princes were more adept at deductive reasoning than serendipity, so the ascribed meaning of serendipity itself is somewhat serendipitous. **2.** Actually, this footnote has nothing further to add. Please return to the main text and carry on reading as though nothing has happened. Apologies for the inconvenience.

LABORATORY RESULTS 1

Courtesy of Experimental Tourist Joël Henry, Strasswalchen, Austria.

♣

O ne thing's for sure, I would never have travelled to Strasswalchen if it hadn't been for Chance Travel. I didn't know that this small Austrian community even existed until I'd consulted the index of my atlas and made a list of the 12 places listed after Strasbourg. Strasswalchen comes third after Germany's Strasburg and Strässa, a Swedish mining site. By a stroke of luck, it comes just before Stratfjord, an oilfield in the North Sea. My destination could just as easily have been Stratford in Canada, New Zealand or upon-Avon if the dice I'd thrown had added up to seven instead of three. Instead of a Shakespearean *Midsummer Night's Dream* or *Tempest*, I was stuck with *The Sound of Music*, for Strasswalchen is in a far-flung corner of Alpine Austria's Salzburger region, where the famous musical was set.

The crisp apple strudels, edelweiss and schnitzels didn't come easy, however. First of all there was the six-hour train ride to Salzburg. Once there, it seemed the entire human race had descended upon this Mozart theme park. Traces of the musically overendowed Salzburger's life were everywhere: a festival, hotel, bar, cinema, exchange bureau, liqueur, chocolate shop and even a flesh-and-bone version complete with wig, bil-

lowing breeches and powdered cheeks. (A good game would be to visit Salzburg in a group and forbid the word 'Mozart' to be uttered during the length of the trip. Those from whose lips the forbidden word escaped would immediately be eliminated or fined – it's a lot harder than it seems!)

Strasswalchen was another half-hour of tortuous winding road from Salzburg, during which journey the mountains were left behind and replaced by a neat and gently undulating countryside. I'd imagined a Hollywood-style Alpine village full of wooden chalets, with a string of snow-topped peaks and glaciers in the background. But no, Strasswalchen turned out to be a small industrial town crossed by a large and very busy motorway. A tour of the town took no longer than an hour, its principal attractions adding up to an unremarkable Baroque church, three *Gasthäuser* dishing up a local cuisine that seemed to have been thrown together from a variety of unlikely ingredients, and a fading theme park with a pasteboard Statue of Liberty, a dwarfish and rusting Eiffel Tower and an unfinished loop-the-loop.

I had brought my walking boots – and would certainly have brought an ice axe as well if I'd had one – ready to *climb ev'ry mountain* that I'd imagined would surround me. But I'd neglected to bring my swimming trunks – what a mistake! Only a few kilometres from the edge of the village lay a magnificent natural lake, the Irrsee – jade-coloured, sprinkled with white sails and surrounded by reeds. I spent a delightful day circumnavigating the lake in the sunshine, taking time out for a little paddle, a siesta on the bank and a small read in a beer garden. *These are a few of my favourite things…*

LABORATORY RESULTS 2: MICRO CHANCE TRAVEL
Courtesy of Experimental Tourist Simon Richmond, Tokyo, Japan.

METHOD: As above, except that you use a local atlas instead of a world atlas.

Some call it chance, but others would say it's fate – and that's certainly how I feel when the dice rolls over. A one would have taken me to the Rosa Kaikan, a cinema in Ikebukero; a three to ROX, a shopping and entertainment block in Asakusa; while four, five and six would have seen me crossing the Sumida River to Ryogoku, the area of Tokyo synonymous with sumo. Instead, I throw a two, which will lead me from my base in Roppongi to Russia, or rather the Roshia Tsusho Daihyobu (Trade Representative of Russia). I can't help but think that a 'higher hand' has tilted the dice towards this destination – the only place I haven't already visited, and symbolic of the country where I have previously travelled so much.

Travelling to Russia by any other means than Chance Travel would require crossing the Japan Sea, traversing China and infiltrating Mongolia. As it is, Russia is a mere two entries down in my street atlas from Roppongi station. Travelling by subway, I will be within easy strolling distance of my goal within half an hour.

> **'Feeling like my Experimental Travels now have the blessing of the Buddha, I head against the tide of commuters with rising anticipation.'**

Outside the subway station, I spy a chubby monk dressed in a brown robe, his straw hat bound with masking tape. He is standing patiently, a bowl in one hand, ready for donations, and occasionally ringing a bell to attract passers-by. My offering of loose change is rewarded with a beaming smile. Feeling like my Experimental Travels now have the blessing of the Buddha, I head with rising anticipation towards the Russian trade outpost, against the tide of commuters.

As I turn the corner beside the Takanawa Tobu Hotel, I pause by a

THE DICE MAN

Written in 1971 by the American writer George Cockcroft, under the pseudonym Luke Rhinehart, *The Dice Man* is the story of a bored psychologist who abandons the usual decision-making processes and lives according to the roll of a dice. Sex, violence, murder and mayhem ensue in Rhinehart's moral vacuum.

The Dice Man quickly developed a cult following and was also banned in some countries. In all the hype surrounding the book, some of the author's philosophical ideas were overlooked. Cockcroft actually tried 'living by the dice' (he met his wife this way), and saw it as a way of overcoming the human ego. He used the dice as a way of embracing life as a series of random events, where no decision was right or wrong. For Cockcroft, living by the dice was also his way of rebelling against the 'seriousness' of a society that was convinced of the righteousness of its own moral superiority.

pair of striking bronze statues: two girls guarding the gate to the Dorf Bluman apartments. Mary Quant miniskirts swishing, these Swinging Sixties chicks hold aloft what could be a torch – or perhaps a cream-filled crêpe. (They're probably old enough to remember the Beatles hit 'Back in the USSR'…) Further along the road is Unicef's Japanese headquarters, its lobby overrun by school kids. I check out the displays detailing the United Nations' work with children around the globe.

Opposite Unicef, a small photography gallery catches my eye. It's empty inside, but the exhibition *Transgender* by Jingu Taeko is a fascinating collection of simple black-and-white images of Michael's decade-long journey to become 'Michelle'. It makes Experimental Travel seem like a breeze in comparison.

My goal now lies a block away on a quiet Tokyo backstreet where youngsters cycle and grannies amble, canes in hand. I can't help but feel a sense of anticlimax. I see a three-storey white building rising in tiers like a giant set of steps. The representative's home lies firmly off limits behind a high concrete wall; its most striking feature is a giant satellite dish on the roof. Discreet to the point of utter anonymity, the building aptly illustrates Winston Churchill's famed quote about Russia being a 'riddle wrapped in a mystery inside an enigma'.

As the Roppongi Station monk himself may have said, sometimes it's the journey that is more memorable than the destination itself. Never has this been made clearer to me than when I took my chances with Chance Travel, throwing a dice to determine my day's outing in Tokyo.

LABORATORY RESULTS 3: COIN FLIP TRAVEL
Courtesy of Experimental Tourist James Broad, London, UK.

METHOD: If you don't have a head for numbers, try flipping a coin instead.

One Friday evening a friend and I arranged to meet at Harrods to see the ridiculously cute animals in the pet shop. To our dismay, the pet department was closed so we were left with no plans and a whole evening to kill. We stood aimlessly on Knightsbridge, neither of us knowing which way to go.

I produced some change from my pocket and suggested that we make a decision based on the flip of a coin. Heads was established as left and tails as right. This worked as a basic rule, but we soon needed to create more guidelines when the first junction approached.

In the space of a few hours we discovered a part of London we'd never visited before, filled with backstreet pubs and cafés, squares and parks. These days city living is very much about chrome bars and gastro pubs, so it was good to find some good old boozers in a part of town that's not known for its down-to-earthness. Having said that, our final destination was a snobby bar on the King's Road, but when you travel by the coin that's just what may or may not happen.

It was amusing to see the reactions of people watching what we were doing. I'm probably the first person in 20 years to produce change from his pocket rather than plastic in Knightsbridge, but I wouldn't advise flipping an American Express card – they can be a nightmare under windy conditions.

CONFLUENCE
SEEKING

HYPOTHESIS: Visit ordered yet random points on the earth's surface.

APPARATUS: A hand-held global positioning system (GPS) device, a detailed map, a compass, a digital camera, a waterproof notebook, a pencil, food and drink, and spare batteries.

METHOD:

1) Find a point where a whole number of degrees latitude (eg 35°S) meets a whole number of degrees longitude (eg 117°E).

2) Travel to it.

3) Document and photograph what you find there.

4) Submit the results to the Degrees Confluence Project website (www.confluence.org).

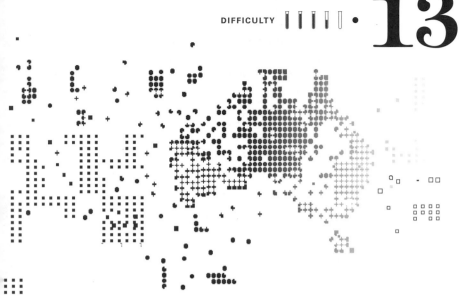

INTRODUCTORY NOTES:

The Degrees Confluence Project (www.confluence.org) is devoted to visiting each of the world's latitude and longitude integer degree intersections, and documenting how these locations change over time, thus creating an 'organised sampling' of the world's confluence points. Alex Jarrett started the project in 1996, because he 'liked the idea of visiting a location represented by a round number such as 43°00'00"N 72°00'00"W'. It also provided him with a use for his newly acquired GPS device.

The Degrees Confluence Project excludes confluence points in oceans and some parts of the North and South Poles. Nonetheless, there are 21,541 of them on land, and more than 12,000 that haven't been visited yet, so there are plenty to hunt down – if you can get to them… Be warned: some of these confluence points are inside restricted areas; others are on mountains or ice; and some have their own unique hazards – like flying golf balls! Wherever you may be, there's probably a point where a line of latitude meets a line of longitude within 80km of you, so you won't need to travel too far. While some confluence seekers like the thrill of the chase, others see it as an exploration – and a celebration – of the utter randomness that results from imposed order.

The project's website has detailed information on how to get the most from your confluence visit. The record number of confluence points has been bagged by Captain Peter, a Sicilian seafarer who to date has visited more than 150 confluences all over the world – from Russia to Argentina.

LABORATORY RESULTS

Courtesy of Experimental Tourist Donna Weston, 35°S 117°E (near Denmark), Western Australia.

❦

V isiting confluence points is like a treasure hunt. The somewhat bizarre goal of trying to find an arbitrary point on the earth's surface really appeals to me and has taken me to places that I would otherwise never have visited.

So far I've made 18 visits to 13 confluences. This time I'm trying to track down the degree confluence 35°S 117°E, near Denmark, on the coast of Western Australia. It's my second attempt at 35°S 117°E, and, accompanied by my friend Sarah, I'm determined to get there!

One of the two most southerly confluences in Western Australia, 35°S 117°E is on the southern side of the Kent River, hiding somewhere in the undulating terrain that's owned by two locals, Tricia and Gordon MacDonald. I have the landholder's details from my unsuccessful first attempt, and call ahead from Denmark to clear permission for us to visit. The owners aren't home, but – luckily – the phone is answered by a man called Robert, who is staying in the house. Robert agrees to take us across the Kent River by dinghy. After making another phone call to clear our visit with Tricia MacDonald, Sarah and I head off along the South Coast Highway towards Bow Bridge.

There's no mobile phone signal down here, so we call Robert from a pay phone to let him know that we're close. Robert sounds a little mystified by what we're doing, but he's reassured by my offer to pick up some tobacco for him.

Robert arrives and takes us down a rough dirt track to the Kent River. I'm glad there's been very little rain, as otherwise the car would have been bogged. It's definitely not a track to try during a normal winter or spring.

Our transport down the river to the MacDonalds' landing is by a motorised aluminium dinghy, called a 'tinny' in these parts. This is Tricia and Gordon's usual means of getting to their property, which is one of only two privately owned blocks on this side of the Kent River. The trip takes 15 or 20 minutes before we pull in among reeds at the wooden landing.

Robert is staying at the MacDonalds' place with his sons Daniel and Joel, and we all head off to our target. There's a huge difference between walking across a level, ploughed paddock and up and down steep, scrubby dunes. We try to follow a reasonably direct route, without much luck, but eventually the distance on the GPS decreases and – counting down the metres – we begin to track 35°S

117°E on top of a ridge. Robert marks a tree with white tape, and we discover that the confluence is in line with the eastern boundary of the MacDonalds' property.

We head back to the house, Robert taking the lead and displaying excellent homing instincts. We share some coffee and then head back to the tinny. Robert proceeds to take off his jeans (with a warning) and wades into the icy water to launch the dinghy. (Meanwhile, Sarah is mumbling about axe-murderers and remote locations.) We chug back up the Kent River, only to run out of fuel just 100m or so from the landing on the north bank, and we have to row the rest of the way.

We leave Robert to dry off, and drive back to Bow Bridge to refill the dinghy's fuel tank and pick up some chocolate for the boys. I am grinning like a coot, immensely satisfied that our visit was successful – and immensely thankful to everyone for helping us so generously with what must have seemed a rather eccentric quest.

'ROBERT SOUNDS A LITTLE MYSTIFIED BY WHAT WE'RE DOING, BUT HE'S REASSURED BY MY OFFER TO PICK UP SOME TOBACCO FOR HIM.'

Photographs taken at degree confluence 35°S 117°E, somewhere near Denmark, on the coast of Western Australia

Counter. tourism

HYPOTHESIS: Do the opposite of what you think a traveller should do.

APPARATUS: A camera. If you're feeling particularly ingenious, try making a pinhole camera.

METHOD: Varies, but could include travelling to a famous landmark and taking a photograph with your back to the sight; alternatively, photograph some tourists practising classical tourism (see the boxed text The Classic Shot, p104). Other ways of practising Counter Tourism might be to take the opposite approach to instruction. If your guidebook advises you to avoid something, deliberately seek it out.

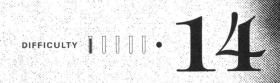

INTRODUCTORY NOTES:

Counter Tourism is not intended as a critique of classical tourism; rather, it's simply an invitation to travel differently. Counter Tourism is a great game to play at key tourist sites, where you may feel most pressured to play the role of tourist and conform to prescribed activities and expectations. Counter Tourism can also turn a negative into a positive: suddenly, all those tourists blocking your view of Big Ben become not an irritation, but a plus.

**Courtesy of Experimental
Tourist Michael Clerizo,
Venice, Italy.**

My instructions for Counter Tourism came directly from the Experimental Tourist guru himself. We spoke to Joël Henry just before my wife and I left London for 10 days in Italy, including a few nights in Venice.

Over the phone from Strasbourg, France, Joël explained: 'When you are in Venice, go to Piazza San Marco. Turn your back to the basilica, put your camera over your head and point it at the basilica. Then take a couple of photos. That is how you do *Contretourisme*. When the photos have been processed, you must have some wine with your friends and talk about the photos with them. This is a very important part of Latourex.'

On our arrival in Venice, heavy rains flooded the city. Workers hurriedly erected the raised wooden walkways that enable people to move around a few inches above the submerged pavements.

But the walkways don't cover every stretch of pavement in town. When you need to reach dry land, such as your hotel or the stairs leading to a museum or the door of a restaurant, you have to make a choice. You can slosh through the water, soaking your shoes, socks and feet, or if you feel particularly athletic you could try leaping to terra firma. Or you can do what the Venetians do, and never leave the house without carrying a supply of carrier bags. When the waters rise, the knowledgeable natives simply slide the carrier bags over their shoes and fasten them with rubber bands. I decided to follow their

'You have done something incredible. You have created the first lost masterpiece of Latourex.'

lead, and the day before we left London I obtained some extra-strong bags from our local greengrocer.

In our hotel lobby, I donned the white plastic bags with blue lettering that reads: 'Tony's Continental, English and Continental Foods, 140 High Road, East Finchley'. My wife said, 'You're not really going out wearing those ridiculous things, are you? I'm very glad we're going in opposite directions. You look absurd.'

She was right, of course. I set out for a day of sightseeing with the bags on my feet and a disposable camera in my pocket, happily impervious to the water. My wife went shopping.

By the time I reached the Piazza San Marco, dusk was settling on the lagoon, the rain had stopped and Venice was starting to dry out.

I followed Joël's instructions but, as I was about to snap my first Counter

Tourism photo, I attracted the attention of a little girl in a 'University of Wisconsin' sweatshirt and baseball cap.

The camera's flash was the girl's cue for a comment to her mother: 'Mommy, look at that man – he's taking pictures backwards.' The girl's mother answered in the unmistakable accent of the American Midwest: 'I've told you before it's not polite to stare at people just because they are doing something different. People over here might laugh at some of the things we get up to in Milwaukee... But God knows why he's got bags on his feet.'

I would love to be able to say that the photos that resulted from my visit to Venice provided many hours of wine-fuelled discussion about Counter Tourism, but in an occurrence that my wife describes as 'typical', I lost the camera.

Joël understood. 'Very sad, very sad,' he said. 'I will tell other Latourex people and everyone will be sad.'

Then he offered me solace. 'You know,' said Joël, 'you have done something incredible. You have created the first lost masterpiece of Latourex.'

THE CLASSIC SHOT

Tourists often get in the way when you're taking photographs, especially when you're one of them. Amsterdam is an ideal setting for Counter Tourism because it's chock-a-block with both icons and tourists.

I began my experiment by observing other tourists' photographic habits, and their very different ideas of what makes a good picture. Initially I felt embarrassed, as if I was invading their party, but I quickly realised that no-one really noticed. I couldn't help but chuckle to myself after I'd taken my shots; it felt cheeky and sneaky at the same time.

I liked my Counter Tourism photos because they are not mere postcard images. I don't just have my own impressions of a place, but those of other visitors too. In Amsterdam, tourists are as much a part of the landscape as the gabled buildings, tulips and canals.

Maya Catsanis, Amsterdam, Holland

LABORATORY RESULTS 2

Courtesy of Experimental Tourist Marika McAdam, Vienna, Austria.

❧

HYPOTHESIS: Subvert the hype of a city by going against the grain.

METHOD: Seek out the antithesis of a city's trademarks. For example, search for the ugly and unromantic in Paris; find a quiet spot in Hong Kong; track down the minimalist and modernist in Mumbai; look for a car club in Venice.

V ienna is much like its women – it is beautiful, but it rarely smiles. Mozart wafts through the air with the smell of French perfume and cigarettes. Doormen wear top hats. Cyclists don't wear helmets. Shoes match bags. Bags match wallets. Even the dogs are designer. The only thing grubby in this impossibly beautiful city is me, and my boots – unfit for the cobblestone streets they traipse.

For a moment I entertain the thought of exchanging my trusty faithfuls for a pair of decadent, pointy-toed Manolos – an idea I quickly abandon (more due to a lack of finance than of materialistic longing), deciding instead to find a place where my boots and I belong. Is it possible, I wonder, to find something *real* in this seductively superficial city? A speedy analysis of the situation brings me to the following conclusions: 1) I need mess; 2) I need disarray; 3) I need shops that sell the simple and practical rather than the ostentatious and useless. And thus my task is set: I will jump on the next Straßenbahn and stay on it until my surroundings no longer make me want to buy clothing I can't afford.

After sitting for an hour and a half in a disturbingly clean Straßenbahn, I am still surrounded by buildings on which half-naked angels recline suggestively with impossible elegance. Enormous architectural pillars of no structural value continue to soar, surrounding me like the bars of some paradisiacal prison modelled on the dreams of Veronese. But just as I am resigning myself to the fact that my boots and I are the ugliest show in town, the tram nears the end of the line…a train station. An ugly one. One with the reassuring hint of urine in the air (probably French, but it still counts).

As if caught up in some kind of force field, I am drawn to a grubby diner nearby. I sip a reasonably priced drink and watch the cast of characters at the bar. There are women whose make-up is more gunky than Gucci and middle-aged men with ambitious ponytails and even more ambitious smiles. There is a real world down here, with litter and loiterers, dreadlocks and drunks, beggars and buskers. French cigarettes are stomped into butts next to chewing-gum stains. Clouds of perfume are chased away by the raucous breeze of the metro, and designer dogs are degradingly muzzled for the city commute. As the glamorous folk from the streets descend the escalators to the underground, they shed their rigidly refined elegance as they go; you can virtually hear the sighs as they let down their hair and let out their stomachs. I belong down here, underground and beyond reproach, far away from the sad side of Vienna's aesthetic bell curve, where comparison and competition are impossible.

But before I am able to celebrate having found a refuge from Viennese beauty, the grimy tunnels of the metro are suddenly transformed into the rich velvet walls of a grandiose opera house and I am plunged once again into a world where I feel underdressed. In this stubbornly sophisticated city, even the buskers play Mozart.

'There are women whose make-up is more gunky than Gucci and middle-aged men with ambitious ponytails and even more ambitious smiles.'

DOG-LEG TRAVEL

HYPOTHESIS: It's a dog's world – see it through their eyes.

APPARATUS: A dog.

METHOD:
1) Find a dog.
2) Let it take you for a walk.

INTRODUCTORY NOTES:

This experiment is inspired by *An Exeter Mis-Guide*, created by Wrights & Sites, a group of performance artists interested in site-specific work, from Exeter in the UK.[1] Drawing on Situationist traditions such as drifting, *An Exeter Mis-Guide* contains a series of 'invitations' for travellers to discover cities within cities. The group uses 'catapult' techniques to jolt travellers into new situations; examples include taking arbitrary bus rides, taking a taxi blindfolded and letting the driver choose a destination, and, as in this case, using a dog to disrupt habitual walking patterns. The group is currently working on *A Mis-Guide to Anywhere* that can be adapted to multiple locations.

As experience suggests that dogs typically follow their usual routes, letting a friend's dog take you for a walk could well provide an insight into your friend's habits and walking tastes. While dogs such as Lassie, Old Yella and brandy-bearing St Bernards have a reputation for rescuing humans from trouble, Dog-Leg Travel could also lead you to it.

1. The original text reads: 'Borrow a dog from a friend. Let it take you for a walk.' For further information, see www.mis-guide.com.

I encountered several unwilling companions before hooking up with my four-legged friend. The stray mutts on the Hopi and Navajo reservations only wanted to roll over or play fetch, and the sheepdog that I took for a walk at the Jackson Hole animal shelter was afraid of men. Finally, just when it was beginning to look like I would never be able to find a willing companion, I serendipitously stumbled onto my canine savior...

It was another quiet evening in southern Montana, as my traveling pardner and I moseyed down to the Two Goose Saloon for bison burgers, a coupla pints of Moose Drool, a few racks of pool and some video keno.

A snow-white malamute was pawing at the bar's glass front door. Snow was

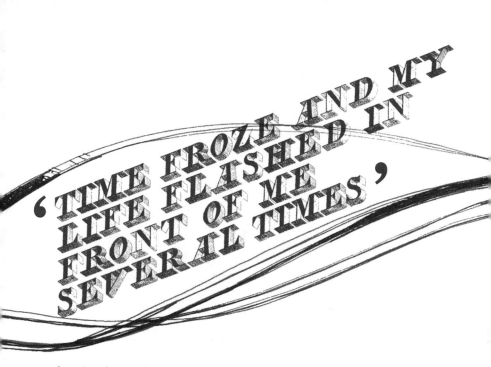

'TIME FROZE AND MY LIFE FLASHED IN FRONT OF ME SEVERAL TIMES'

flurrying down sideways – in the middle of summer! – so the bartender invited the giddy dog inside. Soon enough we were introduced to Oscar, who curled up at our feet to catch our French fry scraps before they hit the floor.

After dinner, we followed Oscar outside for a walk around the one-horse town of Gardiner. First we ambled along to the Yellowstone River. How about a swim? Nope, man, that snowmelt-fed torrent is too cold! Intrigued, we wandered on, pausing at a coupla fire hydrants, en route to Oscar's home base – the front porch of the Continental Divide White Water Company.

Oscar's surprised owners sized me up head-to-toe and then asked if I was a kayaker. 'Nope,' I admitted. 'Good,' they quipped. They explained that they were looking for a guinea pig to accompany a certain greenhorn guide down the river during her inaugural run. Would I care to join them? 'I don't know an Eskimo roll from a Tootsie Roll,' I said. 'Perfect. Show up here tomorrow morning at dark o'clock, sharp.' Oscar howled persuasively. How could I refuse?

My guide Mary had certainly never been down the river before, much less with a client in tow, and I was pretty sure she didn't know how to swim. As I shoehorned myself into my undersized fiberglass shell, Oscar gazed down from the bank with an anxious glint in his aquamarine eyes.

Shortly after we shoved off into the swift current, I mused aloud, 'Shouldn't I be wearing a helmet?'

'Hmm...maybe so,' fumbled Mary.

I flipped over ass backwards in one of the first big rapids. In a breathless panic, I realized I had no idea how to wiggle my way out of the snug neoprene-spray skirt. During what seemed like a lifetime (perhaps a minute and a half?) underwater, gigantic boulders whizzed by my exposed skull. Time froze and my life flashed in front of me several times.

When I finally surfaced, the first thing I saw was an enthusiastic canine scampering down the riverbank. 'He's come to save me,' I enthused. Oscar bravely plunged headlong into the ice-cold river. But instead of heading for me, he made a beeline for the vintage wooden paddle that I had ditched while submerged. In fact, Oscar barely recognized me when I scrambled, coughing and bedraggled, onto the shore. All he cared about was salvaging the paddle for his loyal caretakers.

Back at the Two Goose that evening, Oscar reappeared through the swinging side doors. We stuck to our pints and burgers, lest we be bamboozled into another dawg-inspired adventure.

CHILD-LEG TRAVEL

Can't find a dog? Why not let a child take you for a walk instead? Their owners are often happy to hand them over for a couple of hours, and the child will enjoy the novelty of being the navigator. Note: it's wise to set aside a portion of your budget to spend on child-friendly treats such as ice creams.

Domestic Travel

HYPOTHESIS: Explore another person's world and road test the idea that the grass is always greener.

APPARATUS: Willing friends.

METHOD:
1) Meet up with friends at a café on a Saturday morning.
2) Write your name and address on a piece of paper and attach it to your house keys. Put the keys in an envelope.
3) Mix up all the envelopes and randomly redistribute them among your friends.
4) Spend the weekend at the address in the envelope you are given. If possible, keep the social engagements and appointments made by the usual occupant.

INTRODUCTORY NOTES:

Domestic Travel brings the focus closer to home – someone else's home, that is. This experiment gives you the chance to step into another person's shoes, and test whether the grass really is greener on the other side of the fence – especially if mowing the lawn is on their list of weekend chores. While masquerading as one of your friends for the weekend, you'll not only discover another side of life but also become aware of your own habits and preferences. The most difficult part of this experiment is getting your participants to stick to it – despite the best intentions, this is an experiment that can disintegrate all too quickly.

It's not always easy to see the world through someone else's eyes, something that first-time documentary filmmakers BZ Goldberg and Justine Shapiro discovered when they made a film called *Promises* about Israeli and Palestinian children living in and around Jerusalem. As Goldberg, himself raised in Israel, noted, 'They live no more than 20 minutes from each other, but they are each growing up in very separate worlds.' Shot during the relatively peaceful period between 1997 and 2000, the film explored the conflict through the eyes of seven children aged between nine and 13. All of the children had strong views on the conflict and each other, yet the Palestinian children had never met a Jewish child, and the Jewish children had never met a Palestinian child, nor had they been inside one of the Palestinian camps. During the course of the film, some of the children chose to meet one another; these were moving and enlightening moments as the children struggled to reconcile their fears and prejudices with the reality of wanting to play with their exciting new friend. Sadly, as the years passed, different lifestyles, interests, ambitions – and military checkpoints – proved major obstacles to maintaining their friendship.

Maïa and I began this experiment by scouring the city, tracking down a hundred-odd buildings, houses and streets where we thought we might like to spend 24 hours. Each time we found such a place, we slipped an official Latourex letter of invitation into a randomly chosen mailbox. The letter explained the rules of Domestic Travel and suggested that interested parties should meet us at a café to exchange keys.

On a certain day, at a certain hour, just one couple turned up at the chosen rendezvous: Bernard and Bérengère, a wry and affable couple in their fifties. The fact that they were the only people to have taken us up on our offer simplified things – there would be no need to pull names out of a hat. Their cosy split-level attic apartment on Place du Marché Gayot, in the environs of the cathedral, was something of a botanical garden. They'd left us an entire page of instructions for watering the plants. Thus it was with hose in hand that we explored the apartment.

It goes without saying that the number one rule of Domestic Travel is that the privacy of the usual occupants must under no circumstances be invaded. We didn't require a search warrant, however, to observe that Bernard and Bérengère were nomadic souls. Their interior was furnished in a Moroccan style, and their record collection was hardcore chill-out: yes, Tangerine Dream, Pink Floyd, Amon Düül II. There were metres of books about Ayurveda on the bookshelves, the bathroom could have served as a museum of essential oils, and tucked away behind the fridge – packed with pre-prepared Indian curries – was a glass jar labelled 'Mixed Herbs' filled with Amsterdam's finest.

'Finding even the simplest of objects soon becomes the equivalent of a treasure hunt, often amusing and occasionally annoying.'

Overall, we were left with the feeling we'd committed some kind of a break-and-enter, but there was also a sense of utter disorientation. It's no easy task to get one's bearings in an unknown apartment. Finding even the simplest of objects soon becomes the equivalent of a treasure hunt, often amusing and occasionally annoying. Although our hosts very kindly left us a bottle of wine to welcome us, the bottle-opener was nowhere to be seen. Since they were staying at our place, we needed only to call them. Thus transpired a frankly merciful exchange during which we swapped tips on how to use the microwave, where to find the best bakery in our respective neighbourhoods and which neighbour might lend us a bottle-opener. 'By the way,' added Bernard, 'we can't find the television.'

'I'm afraid we don't own one.'

A long, pregnant pause at the end of the line.

'So how do you fill your time?' he asked. I detected a barely disguised hint of distress in his voice. I was astonished that the simple lack of a television should make him feel as if he'd been condemned to a period of solitary confinement. There was, after all, quite a fine library on offer. I launched into a tirade on the intellectual bankruptcy of television programming.

'I wouldn't go that far,' he said. 'There's cool stuff on TV too, y'know.' And that very night, he said, there was a must-see episode of *Ab Fab* they couldn't bear to miss. So what else could we do? We invited them over.

LABORATORY RESULTS 2

Courtesy of Experimental Tourist Tracey Beavan, New Zealand.

I arrived home two months ago after three years of travel and I was already finding the routine of home a little boring. Luckily, another adventure was calling. Next stop: Domestic Travel!

I contacted six of my closest friends and family and asked if they were interested in spending 24 hours walking in someone else's shoes. The idea was to swap places with a 'not so' stranger and keep all of their appointments and routines from 10am Saturday to 10am Sunday. I was amazed when all six thought it was a fantastic idea, so we booked the weekend.

Since I'd returned from my travels, my friends and family regularly looked at me with what could be described as a combination of admiration and jealousy. They all sang the same song: 'I wish I could do the things that you do' and 'you are so lucky'. It didn't matter how often I explained to them that you need to *want* to do something different to be able to do it; they just wouldn't believe me.

The demise of the weekend started slowly.

First Jennifer purchased a new house and booked the move for that weekend.

Then Jen got roped into an out-of-town trip with work.

Next Kevin asked a girl he had been trying to woo for some weeks out on a date.

And BJ booked a gig for the first time in eight months.

Amazingly, the two people in whom I'd had the least faith were my last two survivors. But then one of my sister Nicole's little girls got the measles.

My mother was the last surviving 'competitor', but as I am currently living with her, it seemed that if we swapped for the day, not much would change.

So the experiment failed – or did it? Perhaps not everyone can let go of their lives for any given length of time to experience something different. I wonder, is it possible that the thing that keeps some people moving is what keeps others stationary?

LABORATORY RESULTS 3: REAL ESTATE TOURISM
Courtesy of Experimental Tourist Martin Robinson, Auckland, New Zealand.

METHOD: Check out a range of 'open for inspection' properties to see how the other half live.

Wanting to see how the other half live, but without swapping lives, I give the re-creations of life in historic homes and museums a miss and trial some real-life 'real estate' tourism instead. Here's how it works: real estate agents run 'open homes' – properties for sale that can be inspected by anyone between certain hours, usually at the weekend. Just pick up some real estate brochures, look through the lists of open homes and plan your own tour.

I live in a modest Auckland abode and my aim is to find out how the 'rich and famous' live. My first stop is Queen Street, and a downtown apartment with a price tag of 'around $500,000'. The views are of multilevel car parks but to compensate there are three TVs. It also has high ceilings and luxury touches, and is perfect if you want to live in an open-plan corridor

('New York loft-style', according to the brochure). I nose around – books by Jeffrey Archer, low-brow DVDs, but some Bob Dylan CDs raise the tone. The jumbo gas barbecue squeezed onto the tiny balcony shows that the traditional outdoor Kiwi lifestyle just can't be fitted into an apartment.

Next is the Auckland version of a Hollywood mansion – a brand-new, architect-designed home for sale in Remuera for $2.5m. For that hill of beans you get five bedrooms, a walk-in room for your clothes to live in, white-marble floors downstairs and thick pile carpet upstairs, a baronial front door and a garage large enough to double as a basketball court. Outside there's a pool, an all-weather barbecue area with a retractable roof and huge heater, and an orchard-worth of olive trees. It's nice, but I decide I want more hectares per buck.

I drive 26km to a horsey lifestyle property. Photographs of horses take precedence over family photos in the lounge room, and the garden has a big swimming pool for horses but only a tiny spa pool for humans. A racetrack surrounds the 15-acre estate, which includes two houses and 24 luxury stables. The agent tells me $1.3m would buy the lot 'and the owner would throw in a couple of horses'. With thoroughbreds costing at least

$20,000, that's a discount worth a new 4WD to go with the rural image.

So, what does life behind the net curtains reveal about Kiwi lifestyles? That cultural preferences are European rather than American or South Pacific, and barbecues are more popular than books. Real estate tourism feeds your lifestyle dreams, gives you a clutch of new design and garden ideas and doesn't cost a cent – as long as you don't fall in love with a home and simply have to buy it.

ero tourism

....

HYPOTHESIS: Discover a city while looking for love.

....

APPARATUS: A partner (lover or friend) and a destination.

....

METHOD: Arrange to take a holiday with your partner. Travel there separately by different means and don't arrange a meeting time or place. Now look for each other...

....

INTRODUCTORY NOTES:

The concept of romantic love hinges on finding the perfect partner. Ero Tourism offers you a chance to find your partner all over again. Joël Henry, who has successfully played Ero Tourism with his wife and collaborator, Maïa, six times in various locations including Heidelberg, Baden-Baden and Nice, says that finding – or not finding – your partner is not necessarily a sign of your success or failure as a couple. Should you fail to meet, you will still have plenty to discuss when you reunite back at home.

Note: newly formed couples should avoid sprawling mega-metropolises such as Shanghai or São Paulo until you know each other a little better.

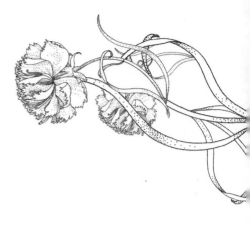

LABORATORY RESULTS

Courtesy of Experimental Tourist Joël Henry, Venice, Italy.

Venice is one of the world's most romantic cities, and thus the perfect place for Ero Tourism. Love is a kind of intimate GPS device that allows separated lovers to reunite, even in the maze that is Venice. Or so I hoped. Having said that, as I disembarked from the vaporetto I didn't hold out much hope of finding my sweetheart, who'd arrived – assuming her train was on time – three hours earlier at Santa Lucia station.

One thing was certain: being agoraphobic, she was unlikely to be among the crowd of tourists feeding the pigeons, having their likenesses digitised on the Bridge of Sighs or fighting fiercely over one of the rare unoccupied tables at Caffè Florian or Harry's Bar. 'Hemingway was here.' Maybe so, but where was Maïa?

The only thing to do was to search for her randomly – at least, almost randomly, seeing as we've been living together for 30 years. Knowing her tastes, I set off to comb the city's art galleries, bookshops and Renaissance churches – the problem being that if she was adopting the same strategy, and exploring my favourite spots, this

'At the Accademia, the driver of a *traghetto* pressed a few euros into my hand in commiseration, but he had no information about the whereabouts of my wife'

could take a while. When we finally bumped into each other I learned that that was exactly what she had been doing – exploring the cafés, bars and restaurants of Venice. The best way to find each other would perhaps have been to look in places we both liked, such as botanical gardens. But there is no such thing in Venice.

We had no means of communication – no mobile phones – but I carried a photo of Maïa with me that I showed amenable Venetians from time to time. They didn't really understand why. At the Accademia, the driver of a *traghetto* (ferry) pressed a few euros into my hand in commiseration, but he had no information about the whereabouts of my wife. I tried to spy her from the Rialto Bridge, an obligatory crossing for anyone visiting Venice, but it's practically impossible to stand still in such a tightly packed crowd – before you know it, you have been carried three streets away.

After a few hours of fruitless searching, a curious thing happened. I started to see Maïa everywhere, and found myself approaching confused women whom from a distance I had taken for her.

Night fell. We'd drawn a blank and my mood was darkening. I imagined my wife being kidnapped by a Venetian prince with sultry eyes, a private gondola and a *palazzo* on the Grand Canal. Thus, fed up and exhausted, I was dragging myself along Calle dei Fabbri in search of a cheap hotel when I suddenly saw her. Her back was turned to me but I knew it was her, seated alone at a table behind the window of a small *osteria*, picking at her plate of *penne rigate* while watching people coming in from outside. My heart beating hard, I knocked on the glass. She turned around sharply, and her eyes locked with mine – and such eyes! It was love at first sight, second time around. Needless to say, we were rather chuffed to have found each other and, together, bring our tour of Venice to an end.

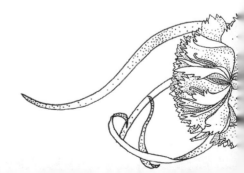

LOVE BIRDS

A number of bird species are known for their monogamous, long-distance unions, of which the Icelandic black-tailed godwits are a shining example. According to a report published in *Nature* magazine, these birds can pair together for up to 25 years (longer than most human marriages), returning to Iceland each spring to breed, but wintering, on average, around 1000km apart. Somehow, without the benefit of email or mobile phones, the birds manage almost without exception to reunite in the same place and at the same time every year. Punctuality is highly prized: birds who fail to appear within a few days of their mate are likely to find themselves 'divorced.'

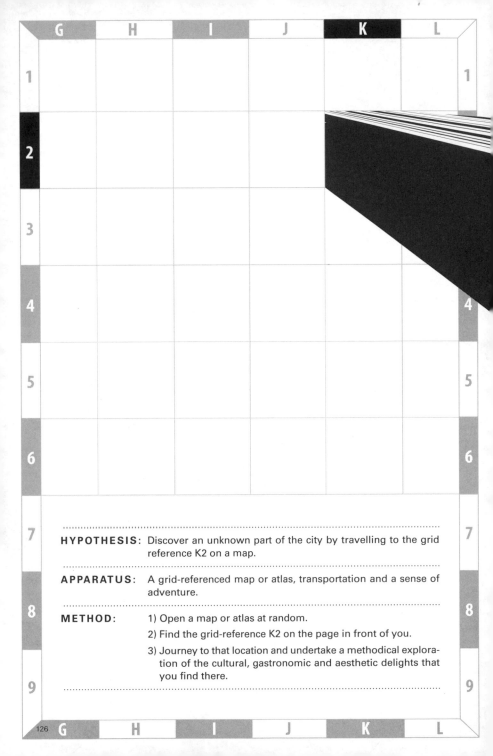

	G	H	I	J	K	L	
1							1
2							2
3							3
4							4
5							5
6							6

HYPOTHESIS: Discover an unknown part of the city by travelling to the grid reference K2 on a map.

APPARATUS: A grid-referenced map or atlas, transportation and a sense of adventure.

METHOD:
1) Open a map or atlas at random.

2) Find the grid-reference K2 on the page in front of you.

3) Journey to that location and undertake a methodical exploration of the cultural, gastronomic and aesthetic delights that you find there.

INTRODUCTORY NOTES:

Expedition to K2 is named after a mountain of the same name in the Karakoram Range in Kashmir. Originally known to Balti-speaking locals as 'Chogori' (the King of the Mountains), the mountain was renamed in 1857 by T. G. Montgomery, a young lieutenant of the British Royal Engineers who happened to be surveying the peaks of Kashmir. Seeing a conspicuously tall mountain towering in the distant Hushe Valley, he named it (one imagines with a flourish) K1 (Karakoram 1); similarly inspired, he labelled the one behind it K2.

Montgomery's monikers clearly lack the pizzazz of the Balti versions; alas, cultural life under British rule was to be sadly lacking the traditional poetics of yesteryear, an oversight that modern-day Bollywood now seeks to remedy. Attempts to scale K2, the world's second-highest mountain, were unsuccessful until 1954. For climbers, K2 remains one of the world's greatest adventures, second only to Everest.

LABORATORY RESULTS

Courtesy of Experimental Tourist Rachael Antony, Melbourne, Australia.

C ompared to the fearsome challenges of scaling K2 in Kashmir, exploring the region of K2 on Map 531 in a Melbourne street directory was decidedly easier, being both frostbite and sherpa free. As I journeyed down the highway I noted that the travel route to K2 would have pleased even the most discerning of aesthetes with a taste for industrial zones. Eschewing the temptation of a seaside stroll (F12) or a visit to the Air Museum (L5), I finally set foot on K2, only to discover that it was pouring with rain. Though I was pelted with rain and bullied by the winds, I remained grimly determined to enjoy K2 to the full – namely, the Cheltenham-Moorabbin Returned Servicemen's League Club, tastefully positioned by Kingston Heath Reserve, a suburban slice of greenery fronting the highway.

I set about photographing the war memorials one invariably finds at an Australian RSL, noting as I did so that the hand of fate had struck down Charles Plowright (1922–43) of the Royal Australian Air Force at the tender age of 21, presumably while fighting in WWII, while his more fortunate relative, Lawrence Plowright (1917–95), had prospered for a full 78 years.

Seeking to escape the elements, I ventured indoors to sample the gastronomic offerings therein and found myself surrounded by snowy-haired senior citizens, a good number of whom were sporting walking frames. Deciding against the sweets and cakes on offer (which appeared to have been 'assembled' rather than 'cooked'), I opted instead for a plain coffee, whereupon I was directed to a coffee machine in the gaming room. Having sought instruction on its usage I sat down to sample my hot beverage while all around me pensioners plunged their savings, coin by coin, into the 'one armed bandits' (aka poker machines).

Finding the atmosphere somewhat depressing, and the coffee entirely undrinkable, I took a short stroll around K2. I paused to photograph a large fibreglass tyrannosaurus rex on display at a garden shop amid children's swing sets and garden gnomes, and then headed home. While the snowy mists of far-off K2 remain a mystery to me, they can surely be no stranger than the flat plains of deepest suburbia.

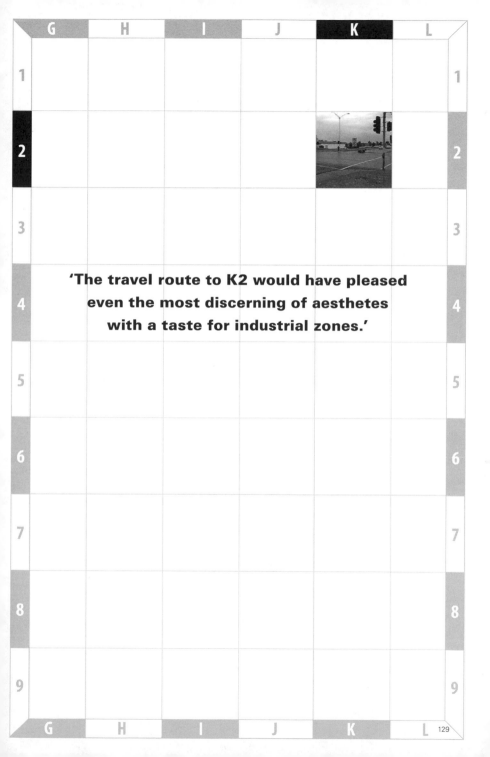

'The travel route to K2 would have pleased
even the most discerning of aesthetes
with a taste for industrial zones.'

Experimental Honeymoon

HYPOTHESIS: Put your marital commitment to the test before the honeymoon is over.

APPARATUS: A wife, husband or equivalent to whom you are willing to pledge your lifelong commitment. The willingness of the aforementioned partner to partake in this experimental journey is highly recommended.

METHOD:
1) Find true love.

2) Propose to the partner of your choice.

3) Get married!

4) Take an Experimental Honeymoon.

Note: the preceding steps are not ranked in order of difficulty.

INTRODUCTORY NOTES:

Marriage is perhaps the most unpredictable experiment of all – who knows how it will turn out? It is not a relationship that can be measured by a rapid-fire litmus test; instead, it is a highly complicated experiment that fuses chemistry, biology and physics (time and space), and evolves slowly over the years.

Wedding ceremonies can often be hijacked by well-meaning relatives who are keen to have their say on flower arrangements, the style and colour of the dress, the invitation list etc. Marriage is further complicated by governments who like to make rules about whom you can marry and how you can do it. And just like the hire car, the dress and the reception, honeymoons can become a status symbol rather than a true reflection of your relationship. Why not break with tradition from the start and do it your own way by taking an Experimental Honeymoon?

By its very nature, an Experimental Honeymoon could take any form you like. For inspiration and ideas, simply check out any of the entries in this book. Like marriage itself, there are no proven rules for a successful Experimental Honeymoon; the only 'rule' is that whatever honeymoon you choose, it must be unconventional. Here we join pioneers of the genre, Ludo and Sasha Jambrich, on a month-long honeymoon in Europe.

LABORATORY RESULTS

Courtesy of Experimental Tourists Ludo and Sasha Jambrich,
Zilina, Slovakia.

How it all started

Everything started with a short journey to Bratislava. Somewhere on the train I lost my mobile phone. Then I lost my umbrella in a tram and forgot a magazine in a restaurant. 'Well,' I said to myself, 'if it is a day to be losing things, let's lose something really valuable.' And so I visited the parents of my girlfriend, Sasha, and asked whether they would agree to me marrying their daughter. They did, and so my freedom was lost too.

And what does a man think about most before his marriage? Stag night? Children? Mortgage? No! The honeymoon. You might think that I would take my sweetheart to an exotic place such as Tajikistan, Madagascar or Guyana. Well, I would have liked to, but fate had another opinion. I had not received a much-needed royalty cheque. I did not get the grant for my new book. Burglars had just cleaned out our apartment, and the insurance company was not eager to pay up. We lacked the resources for even a domestic holiday. I was forced to think of something cheap, interesting and extraordinary (a matter of prestige for a serious traveller). Then it occurred to me that we might hitchhike around Europe for a month, as in my good old student days. And to make it more interesting (and hopefully faster), we would take along a wedding dress. I announced my plan to a somewhat distressed Sasha. What a wonder – fully aware of whom she was going to marry and what she was letting herself in for, she accepted.

Travelling wardrobe

We'll buy a wedding dress for under $10.

Our ad published in the local weekly paper met with unexpected success, and an avalanche of offers rolled in. Our criteria was clear: it had to be long and white, with a veil, perhaps a train and lots of lace.

Seek and you will find. Book an ad and the dress will come. I had to travel about 20km, but I got a dress fit for a princess: snow-white satin with a long train and a veil, decorated with lace and tiny pearls – satin shift included. I even managed to bargain them down to eight bucks.

The gown fitted the bride perfectly, but Sasha did not share my enthusiasm. She thought the dress was too thick, too long, and certainly not very comfortable for hitching. Sadly, she accepted the beautiful garment only after I'd agreed to cut the long train (what a sacrifice!).

Finding the bridegroom's outfit was a much easier task. I had to visit all the second-hand stores in town, but again, I got what I wanted: an almost new black suit with a couple of white shirts from Hugo Boss, a dandy pair of shoes, a Panama hat and a huge silk bow tie pinned with a fake diamond.

Honeymoon suite

Some days later I hit the Internet, keyed the words 'free accommodation' into a search engine, and in a moment got the URLs of several sites whose online members would theoretically offer us a free bed. I sent out a host of emails requesting help for hitching honeymooners. Within a few days I had a mailbox full of answers with dozens of invitations. The problem of accommodation was solved.

The wedding

We packed our backpacks and were ready – or almost. There was just one small detail left. We couldn't start our honeymoon without having taken part in our wedding! And so we were married at the town hall, enduring the speech of a town deputy, the recitation of two poems, the flashes of a photographer, a few tears from the audience and many handshakes and kisses. The ceremony took less than half an hour, and on the whole was painless – but the consequences were to be long-lasting...

Husband and wife

So here we are by the side of the road in our home town of Žilina. As a gallant husband, I offer Sasha my arm. She accepts my gesture with a sweet smile, adjusts her veil and, with love in her eyes, stretches out her right hand and points her upright thumb to the road. To make our intentions clear, we hold up a card with the name of a town in the direction of our destination.

Although I have hitched Europe inside out, I have never tried it in a black suit, with a bride in a white veil by my side. Our activity brings us lots of attention. Some drivers look at us with open mouths, and some with smiles; others shake their heads. A few drivers enter into the spirit of things, sounding their horns, flashing their lights and giving us the thumbs up. Nonetheless, it is seven minutes before the first car stops.

A smiling man who addresses us in Russian sits behind the wheel of an old Nissan. We had wanted to explore Western Europe but, as luck would have it, our first chauffeur comes from the Ukraine. His name is Bogdan. He is going to see his uncle, who lives in the Czech town of Most. The first of our many chauffeurs, Bogdan takes us as far as the Czech border. We exchange addresses and Bogdan invites us to visit him in the Ukraine, promising to slaughter a stag to celebrate our visit.

'Wahnsinn' is German for 'crazy'

Even in conservative Germany, the combination of wedding dress and extended thumb seems to work. On the deserted regional roads we verify the theory that a successful hitchhiker does not need heavy traffic to find a lift. One car is enough. After just a few minutes an elderly Opel stops to gives us a lift. The driver is identical to my idea of the Norse god Odin: long hair, bushy beard and chunky silver jewellery weighing at least 2kg on his arms, ears and neck. It clinks whenever he gives one of his big, roaring laughs. Riding in the back is the owner of the car, an extravagant interior designer complete with perfect, long artificial nails – which Sasha observes with noticeable envy.

'Are you really honeymooners?' the driver asks. '*Wahnsinn!*' – Crazy! Laughing and shaking his head, he says, 'And you are going to travel like this for a whole month? *Wahnsinn!*' He obviously likes our idea very much, and makes a detour of 30km to take us as far as the little village of Hildweinsreuth.

We spend a few days in this wonderful place, enjoying a well-earned rest and sampling barley soup, *weisswurst*, rye beer and other regional specialities. When we leave Hildweinsreuth, our means of transport is a massive truck with a talkative and very opinionated driver. '*Herzliche Glückwunsch!* – All the best for your marriage!' These words welcome us into the cockpit of his Mercedes. Our driver has been driving for more than 30 years, but we are his first hitchhiking honeymooners.

Going Dutch

Getting to Holland is not so easy…

'Wear the veil, please.'

'No I will not.'

'Sasha, wear the veil – nobody stops when you're not wearing it.'

'But it's so hot…'

'Listen, I am not going to stand here until tomorrow. Just wear the veil – I'm wearing my huge bow tie…'

But even the veil isn't helping things too much on the way from Belgium to Holland. The drivers either have no sense of fun or their cars are full of family members. The waiting times stretch to more than an hour in the hot July sun. Nobody wants to give the honeymooners a lift. But finally somebody stops! A young man tries to help us, but he can only take us a few kilometres and leaves us at a terrible place where it is impossible to hitch-hike. Carrying our backpacks, we have to walk a few kilometres to the next highway exit. A real test of our marital commitment.

'Our driver has been driving for more than 30 years, but we are his first hitchhiking honeymooners.'

At night we arrive in Hellevoetsluis, a little town near Rotterdam, where we meet our first Internet host. His name is Aldert, and he is waiting for us. He even gives up his bed for the newlyweds and sleeps in the living room. He has been listed on the Net for more than a year but we have the privilege of being his first guests. The first, but not the last! The next day two Lithuanian girls hitching through Europe also turn up, followed by a hitching Polish couple returning from England.

The capital of unified Europe

The Ardennes always presented a big problem for the armies of warring European powers. But not for us.

We make it from Holland to Strasbourg (France) in nine hours and five lifts, provided by a mechanical designer, a psychologist (who watches the scenery more than the traffic, and we avoid an accident only with the help of God), an Albanian immigrant, a young Frenchman and a bioengineer responsible for the quality of Krombacher German beer (a very important function!).

'Bogdan invites us to visit him in the Ukraine, promising to slaughter a stag to celebrate our visit.'

We arrive at our destination in time for dinner with our new hosts from the Internet, Anne and Michael. Michael is a young scientist who enjoys archery. Anne is responsible for IT in the Strasbourg opera, and collects (and throws) boomerangs. Both of them are into paragliding. And into hospitality too. We have a great time. We cement our friendship and win their hearts via their stomachs. There are lots of berries growing nearby, and we stun their taste buds with pasta topped with blackberries and blueberries. All they can say with their mouths full is, *'C'est bon.'*

Arabian knights
Strasbourg is the last stop on our honeymoon, and it is here that we catch our most exotic lift. A lorry from Tehran. The lorry looks well kept from the outside, but when we get in we find ourselves in the Iranian countryside. The cab is old and shabby, as are its two drivers, Ahmet and Rashid.

Our communication abilities are extremely limited: they do not speak any European languages and we do not have a good command of Persian. So we just smile at each other. They offer us Iranian tea; we treat them with Dutch candies. As we approach Munich, they show us a fax in Arabic script. The only words we are able to make out refer to an office address in Munich.

Their gestures say, 'Do you know this street?'

'Show us the map, and we will find it for you,' we answer with our hands and legs.

'We have no map and no money to buy it...' they reply, using familiar shrugs and gestures.

Now this is what I call courage. Trying to find an address in a city of almost five million inhabitants without a map or knowing a word of the language, and with a 20m truck... Blessed ignorance.

We look up the address on a map in a petrol station and navigate them safely into the hands of the trucking company. This sacrifice costs us precious time, and it is the first night in the whole of our journey that we have to sleep in our tent. At least we have not carried it all this way in vain.

We make our camp in a forest by a petrol station.

Inspector Rex

In the morning we get dressed and take up our position at the station exit. It is half an hour before a VW stops beside us, but the prospective drivers turn out to be representatives of the German federal police. Checking our passports is not sufficient for them: in the hope that they will expose dangerous criminals who are attempting to evade Interpol by cunningly disguising themselves as a newly married couple, the inspector checks our data with headquarters, while the female sergeant keeps a close eye on us. Only that Alsatian sleuth Kommissar Rex is missing! No detection takes place and we are free to go. With a few more lifts, no traffic jams in Austria and no further delays, we are soon back home.

Home sweet home

We store our wedding clothes in the wardrobe, deciding to keep them in commemoration of our honeymoon. Who knows, we may find a use for them on another occasion. It might be interesting to repeat the journey some time in the future. Maybe our golden wedding anniversary...?

THE KINDNESS OF STRANGERS

As Ludo and Sasha have discovered, free accommodation not only helps you save your pennies, it can also open the door to friendship and new experiences. To offer or search for free accommodation options in your city, check out the Internet. These sites will get you started:

www.couchsurfing.com • **www.hospitalityclub.org**
www.place2stay.net • **www.stay4free.com**
www.servas.org • **www.travelhoo.com**

EXQUISITE CORPSE GAD ABOUT

HYPOTHESIS: Let yourself be guided by the collective unconscious.

APPARATUS: A group of friends, a real or virtual piece of paper and a pencil.

METHOD: The first person writes down the name of a destination on a piece of paper. They then fold it over and pass it to the second person, who writes down an activity, folds it over and passes it on. Repeat until everyone has written something down. Possible categories include dress code, budget, duration of travel and theme. When everyone has added a category to the piece of paper, unfold it and see what outing the group has created.

Note: arty types might like to draw pictures instead of words, as the name of this experiment comes from the Surrealist practice of using this method to draw a picture: one person draws the head, another draws the upper body, and so on until the feet. The resulting portrait is an 'exquisite corpse'.

INTRODUCTORY NOTES:

Based on one of the best-known Surrealist games, this experiment is a little like Trip Poker (see p234), in that each individual will be impacted by the decisions of the group, but without the financial risk. Exquisite Corpse is guaranteed to tweak your comfort zone and create some interesting and unpredictable outings. Those of you afflicted by shyness should remember that there's strength in numbers.

While Sigmund Freud developed the concept of the subconscious, it was his protégé Carl Jung who separated the subconscious into the personal (that which is unique to each individual) and the collective (that which is common to all human beings). Drawing on mythology and his own theory of archetypes, Jung argued that the collective unconscious is hereditary – a kind of psychological DNA that we all share, whether we know it or not. Exquisite Corpse allows you to play with the collective unconscious, as the decision of each individual has consequences for the group as a whole, which must adhere to the guidelines it creates.

"OH SURE, MAN RAY MAY HAVE HAD THE JUMP ON US AS FAR AS STYLE GOES, BUT I BET YOU **20** EUROS HE WOULDN'T HAVE HAD THE GUTS TO SHOW UP AT WESTON PARK MAZE IN HIS TOGS"

LABORATORY RESULTS

Courtesy of Experimental Tourists JayBee, the Shagster, MC Andy M, Monkey Trav (with small human assistants Jamie and Alicia) and the Malcoholic, Canberra, Australia.

In a city such as Sydney, New York or Paris, the fun is laid on for you. In Canberra, you have to make your fun yourself. Could there thus be a better place to play Exquisite Corpse? When I emailed four of my friends with the preposterous suggestion that they give up their Sunday afternoon to go on a trip to god-knows-where to do god-knows-what, they answered as enthusiastically as if I'd suggested we go see the White Stripes play a free show. (Note: that would never happen here.)

When the Surrealists wanted to get a game of Exquisite Corpse together, they folded up pieces of paper in smoky cafés, sipped absinthe and mused on the role of the subconscious in revealing the nature of self. In contrast, me and my mates shot a few emails around on company time while wondering whether to wander over to the mall and check out the 'Valley Girl' sale. A compilation of our Surr-emailist correspondence revealed the following itinerary:

Destination: Weston Park maze (a kiddies' playground on the shores of Canberra's blue-green–algae infested Lake Burley Griffin)

Activity: synchronised swimming

Dress code: primary colours only

Item to bring: a small soft toy with a cute name

Budget: $22 each

Oh sure, Man Ray may have had the jump on us as far as style goes, but I bet you 20 euros he wouldn't have had the guts to show up at Weston Park maze in his togs.[1]

At 4pm sharp on a sunny Sunday we rock up to the maze – a tumbledown structure of 6ft-high pine logs – clutching our soft-toy pals (Ignatz, Kommissar Brustwarzen, KittyTeddy, Horatio and Tinkles) and wearing our togs over our clothes. Nonplussed, the kid on the admission stand acts like he sees this kind of thing every day.

'Are you a family?' he asks.

'Are we ever!' I reply.

'Right. That's $14 for the lot of you, then,' he says.

You beauty: we're going to do the job and have beer money to spare!

1. Swimming costume.

Monkey Trav has brought the offspring with him. Jamie (aged seven) and Alicia (aged four) are old hands at this maze business, and start tugging on Dad's arms. 'C'mon!' pleads Jamie, 'I KNOW THE WAY!'

'That's not the way,' says the attendant. 'You should go in the door marked "IN".'

What a smartarse. Instead we follow Jamie's lead. Fifty-two dead ends later, we reach some kind of an open area.

'Okay, guys, let's synchronise!' I wave my arms around enthusiastically to get them all fired up.

'Do we have to?' pleads the Malcoholic.

'Quit whining and start swimming. Act as though no-one is watching!' I tell him.

Of course, just as the Shagster is imploring us to 'get your bums closer together!', some kids walk round the corner asking, 'Did one of you guys drop a mouse?' I sheepishly reclaim Ignatz and get back to some synchronised backstroke.

Task complete, we follow Jamie to the 'OUT' door. Congratulations ensue. MC Andy M demands a drink. At the kiosk, empty soft-drink bottle in hand, I ask the girl who's serving if she has a bin.

'No, there's no beer,' she says.

She must have heard my subconscious speaking.

EXQUISITE PROMENADE

As an alternative, Joël Henry suggests that travellers take an Exquisite Promenade. Decide upon a walking itinerary and break it up into sections, according to the number of participants. Allocate a section of the walk to each participant, and walk it – either in sequence as a relay or at random. In the end, the entire walk will have been completed, but no-one will know its entirety.

fly by night

HYPOTHESIS: Discover a town by night.

APPARATUS: Transport to your destination and lots of stamina.

METHOD: Travel to your chosen destination, arriving in the evening. Spend the night exploring the town and its surroundings until the sun rises, then return home.

Note: while this experiment offers a good excuse to explore a city's nightlife, it doesn't have to be the focus of your trip – thinking laterally may yield more interesting results.

INTRODUCTORY NOTES:

Musicians Paul Simon & Art Garfunkel may have referred to it as their 'old friend'[1] but the novelist Joseph Conrad summed it up with his iconic title *Heart of Darkness*. Night is nothing more sinister than the natural consequence of day, and yet it is a place that humans have populated with the deepest fears of their imagination: ghosts, werewolves, vampires and evil spirits. The city is a different place by night. After midnight, when the world is sleeping, the restaurants are closed and the entertainment district winds down, exploring it can seem like a daunting task, requiring you to brave both your real and imagined fears.

1, To be precise, 'Hello darkness my old friend, I've come to talk with you again'; 'Sound of Silence' from the album *Sounds of Silence*, 1966.

'I suddenly feel less like an adventurer, and more like a target'

The road to Boulder, Utah, is one of the most beautiful – and treacherous – drives in North America's desert southwest. Red-rock cliffs and vast expanses of undulating Navajo sandstone stretch from horizon to horizon – so big, it's impossible to judge distance. But Highway 12 is only 20ft across, without a guardrail, as it traverses a razor-thin ridgeline that drops precipitously on either side into bottomless gorges and canyons. Locals call this the Hog's Back. One false move behind the wheel, one lingering look at the jaw-dropping scenery, and you're a goner. Far below, the tiny town of Boulder (population 180) spreads out along a verdant valley, a peaceful oasis in an otherwise forbidding landscape that the government has classified as not even rural, but frontier.

I arrive at twilight and see that there's no real business district along Boulder's mile-long main drag – just a few houses, a motel, several shops, a restaurant and a café, all separated by swaths of pastureland. There are no bars or pubs – this is Mormon country, after all. I pull into the 12-room motel, and the manager gives me a hand-drawn map of Boulder. A single U-shaped road connects one end of Main St to the other. Along it there's a post office, town hall and Mormon temple. That's it, the whole town.

At around 10pm I set out to explore, feeling like an adventurer, ready for discovery. Southern Utah's night sky is jam-packed with a million twinkling stars. I stare up at the Milky Way as I walk along the double-yellow line of deserted Main St, my footsteps the only audible sound. Except for a couple of streetlights, everything is in darkness. I saunter past the post office to the town hall, where I cup my hands on the glass to see inside. Nothing. I do the same at a curio shop and the Mormon temple. Can't see a thing.

I reach the edge of town and the beginning of the rugged red-rock frontier. Provoked by the noise of my footsteps, a dog barks viciously in the dark. Adrenaline courses through my veins.

I hold my breath and look for the animal, but can't see into the blackness. I suddenly feel less like an adventurer and more like a target, easy prey for some unseen force – a ruffian, a wild animal, a ghost. A chill runs through me. It occurs to me that I may not be alone, that I've been ambling along, talking to myself, peering into dark windows, not even bothering to look over my shoulder. The dog persists. A light comes on in a house. It must be its owner waking up. I burst into a sprint and tear off down Main St. Get me out of here!

Back in my motel, I turn off the light and stare out at the stars. The constellations are all that's worth seeing in Boulder tonight. As for the rest, I'll check it out tomorrow, when the dogs and goblins retreat from the searing noonday sun.

BARCELONA BY NIGHT

I feel as though I have 'lost tourist' printed all over my forehead as I desperately try to find the dog-eared page that contains the map of Barcelona. Touts push matchbox-sized flyers into my hand as if they are drugs. 'Rooms for rent, Cheap Accommodation. Phone Now!'

This is certainly a trip with a difference. I am to spend the next 12 hours wandering around Barcelona until the first flight home. It occurs to me that this experiment could suit someone who works nine to five and wants to keep the travel bug at bay. And thanks to the expansion of budget airlines, the usual night out with friends could be spent in, say, Paris, instead of down the local pub…

It feels good not to be lugging around a heavy suitcase, to be able to bypass the conveyor belt and breeze towards the airport's exit. I'm initially a bit daunted by my task, but my nerves settle once I get going. I've promised myself not do anything stupid (eg wander into dodgy areas or drink way too much), and I am taken over by the excitement of the experiment.

As my evening in Barcelona unfurls, my Fly by Night 'stay' basically consists of a lot of bar and café hopping. I make friends with some Spanish students and a lone Norwegian, and see a side of Barcelona I might not otherwise have experienced. But honestly, as the sun rises and I head back to the airport, my last thoughts are for my bed.

Maria Castillo-Stone, Barcelona, Spain

re like a target

less like adventurer

horse
head
adventure

Hypothesis:	Test normal standards of social behaviour and etiquette by drawing attention to yourself in an outlandish and potentially absurd manner.
Apparatus:	Some form of strange prop or costume, eg a horse's head.
Method:	Don your costume and venture into society. Gauge people's reactions: do they engage with you, laugh at you or turn away and pretend they haven't seen you? See Slight-Hitch Travel (p204) for suggestions that combine this form of travel with hitchhiking.

INTRODUCTORY NOTES:

As a traveller, you often stand out – you look different, you dress different and you probably 'speak funny', or not at all. You're often doing the wrong thing in the wrong place and relying heavily on the kindness of strangers (and your miming talents) to get you through the day.

Standing out and appearing unusual is an accepted part of travelling, but British comedian Mark Butler took things too far when he decided to wear a horse's head in Japan. Without context and without reason, Butler transgressed the accepted bounds of the eccentric and entered the no-man's-world of the strange. Butler expected his horse's head to be a talking point, but it didn't go quite as planned. More provocative than most of the games in this book, you can be sure this experiment will have unpredictable results.

Funnily enough, while we may be inclined to stare at those who stand out in a crowd, we'd rather turn a blind eye to things that make us feel uncomfortable: the homeless, the physically impaired, the accordion busker seeking your loose change…

LABORATORY RESULTS

Courtesy of Experimental
Tourist Mark Butler,
Tokyo, Japan.

⟜⟜❧

In an experiment to test Japanese reactions to abnormal behaviour, I have decided to travel around Japan wearing a rather eye-catching white horse's head. This type of eccentricity in a land that is known for its strict conformity produces some interesting results – I become invisible. From the boutiques of Tokyo's fashionable Ginza district to the freezing slopes of the ski resorts in the west of the country, I travel unseen, unnoticed. Stand out too far in this country of uniformity and you appear to blend in, for the extreme cannot be seen.

'As you might imagine, it's not easy snowboarding while wearing a horse's head.'

In the Winter Olympics city of Nagano the snow is fresh and relentless and it's time for this white horse to take a gallop on the famous Happo-one slopes. The snowboarding is my real reason for coming here; the equine antics are just a sideline. But when

the ski lifts are full and the queue is long, a horse's head proves to be the perfect accessory for queue-jumping. No-one is up for a confrontation with a horse, and there are no raised eyebrows, no interaction of any kind. Social politeness combines with voluntary blindness, and the result is a society that's perfect for overconfident foreigners to abuse.

As you might imagine, it's not easy snowboarding while wearing a horse's head and I soon tumble to the ground.

Offers of help are rare on ski slopes nowadays, but dressed as I am there are none. But then I hear some familiar English words, and the cry 'Get out of the way, you dickhead!' brings me to my feet.

Within seconds I am surrounded by a group of Australians, all screaming, 'Hey look! It's a horse!' None of them feels the need to ask 'Why?' It's nice to be noticed at last. 'You should be careful,' one of them warns; 'they eat horse sashimi in this prefecture.'

But not in my hotel. The only raw horse here is my grazed skin, where I had fallen.

A few days later and I am back on the train to Tokyo, attracting unwanted stares from frozen schoolchildren who are forced to wear shorts in the winter. Without my animal attachment, I too feel vulnerable. I have become visible once again.

A mother spies my snowboard and we strike up a conversation in pidgin English. She asks me if I visited Hakuba, and I tell her that I did. She takes out a pen and paper, and explains how the resort got its name. 'The first character, *ha-ku*, means white,' she says. 'The second character, *ba*, means horse. Because the mountains look like a horse shape.' Perhaps this explains why I wasn't so noticeable after all.

MAKING AN ASS OF YOURSELF

Travelling while disguised as a horse has traditionally had mixed results. The world's first novel, *The Golden Ass*, written by the ancient Roman Lucius Apuleius, recounts the bawdy adventures of a young aristocrat who is intrigued by magic. During the course of his travels, he stumbles across a potion that will transform him into a bird. Thanks to a magical mishap he is instead transformed into an ass, whereupon he is taken by bandits and a new set of unpredictable adventures begin.

♖ ♟ HUM♟N

HYPOTHESIS: Explore a city through the eyes of a chess piece.

APPARATUS: A mobile phone and a black or white T-shirt (costume optional).

METHOD:

→

1) Assemble players.

2) Find a city grid to use as a board.

3) Nominate the 'controllers' and assign the remaining positions.

4) Play chess.

Note: the chess game is played by having two controllers at a home base playing a normal game of chess. Using mobile phones, the controllers text or call each of the live players and inform them of their next 'move'.

CHESS

INTRODUCTORY NOTES:

Human chess is a form of psychogeography (roughly described as the study of the geographical environment and its effects; see p23). By mapping the board onto a city grid, we are exposed to areas we would otherwise never visit, in a way that we wouldn't usually experience – just how does the city look through the eyes of a pawn? Human Chess also explores how different cities function as a chessboard, and how the experience of the game changes the urban landscape. Plus you get to test the reactions of passers-by – what do they think of a bunch of people in chess costumes running around the central business district?

Note: you don't need to fill all the positions, as players can be reassigned to new roles as they are captured. Different pieces will have different experiences: centre pawns can expect to be taken early; pawns at the side of the board may never move; and queens will zip all over the place. Don't forget that playing human chess is thirsty work, and can take a couple of hours – make sure your board includes somewhere you can discuss strategies over a drink or two afterwards.

'AN ATTRACTIVE WOMAN WALKS BY. ONE OF THE BISHOPS WONDERS IF SHE IS INTERESTED IN CHESS. IF SO, I WONDER IF SHE HAS EVER HAD ANY FANTASIES ABOUT THE BLACK KNIGHT? BOTH BISHOPS EXPRESS REGRET THAT THEY ARE MEN OF THE CLOTH.'

PAC-MANHATTAN

Providing your city has a central grid of streets you can play any game you like, from Chinese Checkers to Space Invaders. If you're looking for something a little quicker than chess – and much more energetic – how about adapting a quick game of Pac-Manhattan? Dressed up as Pacman and ghosts, players run around the streets of Manhattan in full costume, guided by players with mobile phones.

According to the PacManhattan project's Mattias Romeo, the game is 'utterly exhausting'. And what response can a bunch of guys sprinting down New York's streets dressed up as video game characters from the 1980s expect from passers-by? 'Not a ton,' Romeo says. 'New Yorkers are a famously jaded bunch.'

For more information, check out www.pacmanhattan.com.

LABORATORY RESULTS

Courtesy of Experimental Tourist Sharilyn Neidhardt, Williamsburg, USA.

᪥

O rchestrating human chess is a massive organizational effort. I spend the three weeks before each game posting to online bulletin boards, sending emails and attempting to assign the roles to volunteers. I also select a neighborhood and design the game board. I get in touch with local papers as well as coffee shops, bars and other businesses in the area to call their attention to what we are doing.

Even if I don't get all 32 pieces covered by volunteers, or if enough people don't turn up, we play the game anyway. I've managed to fill every single piece on the board only once, and that was the first game I organized, on Manhattan's Lower East Side.

The game is operated from a nominated home base, usually a park. Two players – usually me and another person – play a chess game on a regular board. Following each move, we use a mobile phone to call each human chess piece and tell them what to do.

Each human chess piece has a map of the neighborhood showing which intersection corresponds to which square. When I call the white bishop (for example) and tell her to move to B5, she can look on her map and see that she needs to walk to the corner of South Fifth and Bedford Ave.

At the beginning of the game we usually reassign pieces that have been captured, since there are always a few vacant roles. During the endgame, we start funneling captured pieces to a social venue, usually a bar somewhere on the game board.

I think Human Chess is more interesting for the pieces than the controllers, for whom the game is not so different from any other one, except that there's a lot more people involved. Human Chess pieces have written about their experiences, which you can find on my website (www.humanchess.typepad .com/project/). For instance, one knight has written: 'An attractive woman walks by. One of the Bishops wonders if she is interested in chess. If so, I wonder if she has ever had any fantasies about the Black Knight? Both Bishops express regret that they are men of the cloth.'

LITERARY JOURNEY

HYPOTHESIS: Travel around the world via a bookshelf.

APPARATUS: You will need a bookshelf containing books, plus a pen and paper to keep track of your journey.

METHOD: Choose a book from the bookshelf and commence reading. Continue reading until a foreign country is mentioned in the text. Then choose a second book that's somehow related to that country and begin reading again. Repeat until you have either returned to your point of origin or have completed one circumnavigation of the globe.

INTRODUCTORY NOTES:

As any great reader knows, the journey of the mind is the greatest voyage of all. Regardless of where you are or the state of your finances, Literary Journey gives you a ticket to ride – even though your physical destination may be no further than your nearest bookshelf or library. Literary Journey not only gives you the opportunity to explore unknown (and familiar) regions, it is also the only Experimental Travel game in this book that allows you to travel through time. Whether your interest is in revolutionary Russia, 14th-century China or prehistoric France, you can travel there with the help of a book – and a little imagination.

Courtesy of Experimental Tourist David Prater,
Melbourne, Australia.

W hen I was at school, the librarian used to force us to engage in USSR (Uninterrupted Sustained Silent Reading). Though the Soviet Union may be dead, I approached this experiment determined to prove to myself that the world of literary travel is glamorous, exciting and relevant. And so it was that, quietly, respectfully and in the spirit of complete bookishness, I decided to travel around the world using nothing but other peoples' words.

I began my journey at the top left-hand corner of my own bookshelf, where I found **James Joyce's *A Portrait of the Artist as a Young Man***. Thus my object would be to return to **Ireland** within an arbitrarily decided number of books (10) or else circumnavigate the world using Joyce's *Bildungsroman* (coming-of-age novel) as my starting point. I settled into a comfortable armchair and began reading, thinking it might be several hours or hundreds of pages before I received a hint about my next stop.

> warm smell! Dante knew a lot of things. She had taught him where the Mozambique Channel was and what was the longest river in America and what was the name of the highest moun- ...ll knew more than Dante because

Not so: on page five a reference to the **Mozambique Channel** sent me scurrying for my atlas. Unfortunately, I possess not one book either by, for or about Africa – let alone Mozambique. I needed to think fast, as I was already 'literally' on a plane from Dublin, heading south for the great continent. My solution was **Craig Werner's *A Change is Gonna Come***, a history of African-American music. Close enough. I started reading, and on the sixth line of the first page I received my next destination: **Vietnam**.

Things started happening pretty quickly after that. From **Neil Sheehan's** *Two Cities: Hanoi and Saigon* it was a short and perhaps predictable step to **France**, and **Jean Genet's** *Our Lady of the Flowers*. This sent me ricocheting across Europe to **Germany**, courtesy of **Günter Grass'** *Local Anaesthetic*. That book's first page directed me to **Alexandria**, Egypt, where I came across another problem not unlike that posed by the Mozambique stopover. I had nowhere to get off my 'plane'.

'My flight route was beginning to look like a child's drawing – a series of red lines hastily scribbled across the globe. Would I make it back to Ireland in time for tea?'

I settled on **Paul Bowles'** *The Sheltering Sky*, set in Morocco, or somewhere near it. The Sahara in any case. Not too far from the Nile. I wouldn't be staying long, however: no sooner had I sat down to read from Bowles' dreamlike novel than I was promptly ordered to catch the next plane to the **United States**, where I picked up a copy of Nicholson Baker's *The Size of Thoughts*. I feared for a moment that this philosophic and reflective set of essays might prove to be my Waterloo, leaving me bogged down and unable to continue moving.

movement, and it smelled of stale wine and urine. At the table in the darkest corner sat three Americans: two young men and a girl. They conversed quietly, and in the

I need not have feared. After about 10 pages I was offered a chance of escape via Lake Ontario. Ah, Canada! If only I was a Margaret Atwood fan. This stop, therefore, proved a dead end. I continued with Baker until he made a reference to **New Zealand**. Okay, this was more like it! From Ireland to Mozambique to Vietnam to France to Germany to Morocco to the USA to New Zealand. And all within about 30 minutes' reading time. My flight route was beginning to look like a child's drawing – a series of red lines hastily scribbled across the globe. Would I make it back to Ireland in time for tea?

... Polynesia, which in New Zealand.

LIBRARIAN'S TIPS

An alternative, and perhaps more conventional, approach to this experiment is to read each book from cover to cover. To create an itinerary, simply choose your destination – the Middle East, for example – and start tripping around the region via its literature.

For serious literary frequent-flyer miles, start with an author from your country, then read a book by someone from a neighbouring country and continue until you make your way around the globe. Note: this long-distance read will require around 193 books.

this they endeavour'd to get away, upon which I order'd a Musquet
to be fir'd over their Heads, thinking this would either make them
surrender, or jump overboard; but here I was mistaken, for they

⁶ Tupia was a native of (Tahiti,) who had accompanied the expedition when it
.... on July 13, 1769. There is one basic language ....

My fate ended up in the hands of Captain Cook himself. A
copy of **Cook's Journals**, written while in Aotearoa, furnished me with an opportunity to island-hop my way north
to **Tahiti**. This left me no choice but to begin reading **Bengt**
and **Marie-Thérèse Danielsson's** impassioned history of
nuclear testing in the Pacific, *Moruroa, Mon Amour*. They
promptly sent me to **England**. This was fine by me: nine
books down, and I was almost back where I started.

chairs, and live in stone houses – in other words, to live ....,
like the English lower middle class, from which the missionaries
had sprung. Consequently the natives needed money, and in
.... they had to plant ...

Unfortunately, the next book on my shelf by an
Englishman happened to be Thomas Hardy's *Jude
the Obscure*, in whose Wessex setting I found
myself whiling away the rest of the afternoon. I
never did make it back to Dublin, but then again I
did manage to see quite a bit of the world. I also
realised that I need to revamp my book collection.

My journey ended up as a real *tour de force*, not unlike a
Tom Clancy novel. It's an exercise that might come in
handy if you are already overseas, perhaps staying with
a friend, and the weather outside is so foul that you cannot possibly leave the house. An afternoon spent touring
the globe via your friend's book collection could be just the
ticket. And a very cheap ticket at that.

lyrical
tourism

Hypothesis:	Explore a city via the lyrics of a famous song that pays tribute to it, using the words as both itinerary and travel guide.[1]
Apparatus:	A collection of timeless musical paeans to particular cities, a handy transcription of their lyrics, and some frequent-flyer miles.
Method:	Compile a list of classic songs about specific cities ('New York, New York', 'I Love Paris', 'Chicago' etc). Pick one of the songs at random and travel to the city in question, re-creating the various places, scenes or moods described in the song.

1. For a variation on this theme, see Opus Touristicus (p188).

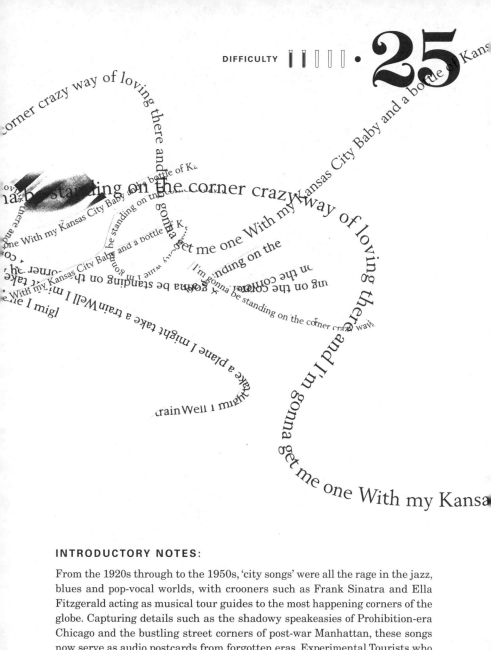

INTRODUCTORY NOTES:

From the 1920s through to the 1950s, 'city songs' were all the rage in the jazz, blues and pop-vocal worlds, with crooners such as Frank Sinatra and Ella Fitzgerald acting as musical tour guides to the most happening corners of the globe. Capturing details such as the shadowy speakeasies of Prohibition-era Chicago and the bustling street corners of post-war Manhattan, these songs now serve as audio postcards from forgotten eras. Experimental Tourists who follow the tunes' trails will receive an insightful glimpse into a town's storied past, as well as a first-hand look at how urban areas change over time.

"I needed to go to Kansas City, Missouri, and find a crazy little woman, who would administer a 'crazy way a lovin'.'"

Courtesy of Experimental Tourist Chris Baty,
Oakland, California, USA.

The fates picked 'Kansas City' for me, the R&B standard written by Jerry Lieber and Mike Stoller and popularized by Fats Domino. The travel instructions provided in the song were clear: I needed to go to Kansas City, Missouri, and find a 'crazy little woman' who would administer a 'crazy way a' lovin'. Both of us would then need to procure a bottle of 'Kansas City wine' and make haste down to the corner of '12th Street and Vine'.

Thankfully, my 90-year-old grandmother lives in Kansas City. Bearing a feisty temperament, diminutive stature and increasingly unreliable memory, she seemed aptly cast in the role of my wild-eyed Kansas City woman. After arriving in KC, I made a quick detour to the liquor store for a bottle of locally produced hooch, at which point my grandma and I set out towards downtown Kansas City in search of 12th St and Vine.

Some pre-trip research clued me into the fact that 12th St and Vine had once comprised the lawless northern tip of Kansas City's rollicking jazz district. Today's 12th St and Vine has been reduced to a street sign set in the middle of a vacant lot, the infamous nightclubs (and 12th St itself) having been replaced by expanses of low-income housing projects.

The neighborhood was quiet as we parked across the street from the one-time epicenter for jazz-age indulgence. I uncorked the wine, and my grandmother and I choked down cups of the noxious stuff for the sake of historical accuracy, keeping an eye on the grassy patch for signs of adventure.

'Is it somebody's birthday?' my grandmother asked eventually, having finished her wine and forgotten what we were doing there. After a few more minutes, I decided to let the sleeping ghosts of Kansas City's musical past continue their slumbers unmolested, and we turned the car around and headed home.

MASCOT
TRAVEL

Hypothesis:	See the world through the eyes of a mascot.
Apparatus:	A mascot of your choice and a camera.
Method:	Pick a personal mascot and take it on your travels with you, eg a stuffed toy, pet rock or garden gnome. Take its picture outside famous landmarks and record its other experiences with a camera. On your return home, consider making a photo album of your mascot's travels. Show it to your friends. The album should look like you were never there.

INTRODUCTORY NOTES:

A spontaneous purchase, a flash of inspiration, a love of travel and nostalgia for the road prompted a whimsical journey that took photographer Willy Puchner and his beloved penguins, Sally and Joe, on an adventure around the world, now immortalised in a number of publications.[1] Joe is 45 inches (114cm) tall and weighs just over 12 pounds (5.5kg). Sally is 43 inches (109cm) in height and weighs exactly 11 pounds (5kg). Their bodies are made of polyester, and after every journey they get a fresh coat of colour. For the most part they travel by car or are carried around in specially constructed backpacks. Since 1988 Puchner has photographed the penguin couple posed in front of the world's best-known travel spots – from Egypt's pyramids to Mexico City – receiving all kinds of reactions along the way:

> We got the most impulsive reactions in New York: cars followed us and honked their horns, pedestrians stopped and applauded. And it was there that we had another wonderful experience… I got into an elevator with Joe and Sally to go up to the 40th floor of a skyscraper and take a picture from its scenic terrace. About 30 persons could fit into the elevator, 25 were already inside, and we managed to squeeze in, facing the door. The penguins were looking towards the people behind us. There was a ghostly silence. Suddenly someone started to chuckle, and then someone else couldn't hold it in any longer. By the time we got to the 40th floor, everybody was laughing at the top of their lungs. We couldn't see the people because we had our backs to them. We got out, the doors closed behind us, and the elevator continued its ascent.

The penguins represent a sense of nostalgia for Puchner, and are symbolic of his yearning to travel and his desire to evade mortality. Whatever mascot you choose, and regardless of its meaning for you, you may find that this particular experiment takes you on a longer and deeper journey than you first anticipated.

1. Titles include *Joe & Sally: A Long Way from Home* (New York: Penguin USA, 1993) and *Penguins – Traveling the World: The Long Road Home* (London: Könemann UK, 1999). To learn more about Willy Purcher see his website: www.willypurcher.com.

Courtesy of Experimental Tourist Kanani Fong, Grand Canyon, USA.

The writer's world is alternately small and large, then small again. Hula Girl sits on my bookshelf as a reminder that when my prose becomes jumbled, my imagery blurred, sometimes the only solution is distance.

For me, Hula Girl is symbolic of deeper meanings. I am Hawaiian by blood, but when I was growing up it was difficult to reconcile the pride I felt as a Hawaiian with the reduction of our culture to trinkets: plastic leis, hula girls, musicians playing the ukulele, and – most baffling to me – an expectation of the exotic. I never had the sense that who I was or what my family did was exotic. My uncle was a plumber on the isle of Kauai; my auntie sang on the Fern Grotto Cruise. This was just who they were, what they did.

I knew there were struggles within my culture, but no-one wanted to hear about them. The 'foreign' culture just wanted a hotel, a hula show, a lei greeting at the airport and a luau. But this is now changing; our language has returned, and today our chants, dance, the making of leis and the telling of stories are all performed with an understanding of what they mean, not just how they look or because they are thought to be 'exotic.'

Travel is a transcendent experience. It helps me move beyond the expecta-

tions I've set for myself. Hula Girl is an icebreaker. People see me setting up a shot, and then they come and talk to me. It's that connection, hearing what people have to say or think, finding something to smile about, which gives me good memories of my trip and deepens my understanding and appreciation of life.

So Hula Girl and I travel. With the click of a key, we go to the Grand Canyon on the once golden Route 66. It was a road that passed through many places; however, rarely were any of them the final destination. Bobby Troupe immortalized Route 66 in a song. It connected Chicago to LA, winding through mountains, over plains, across deserts, ending at a palm-lined beach on a pier with a Ferris wheel. Now, the desert is reclaiming this road. Weeds grow through the asphalt, and like a joke, a sign that reads 'For Sale $300' has been posted on a hollow trailer with rusted cars dumped around it. But there is beauty, too. Ocotillo blooms red like a paintbrush, thunderheads rise above the mesa, and there are stretches where the sky is the horizon's bonnet.

Newberry Springs, Oatman, Kingman, the Hualapi Reservation, Seligman, Ash Fork and Williams survive because they have gas stations, trinket

'SO HULA GIRL AND I TRAVEL.'

shops, diners, museums and burros. The people are more sturdy than the sainted road, thin on nostalgia but with good hearts, and as mysterious as the tumbleweeds in the landscape.

'Hula Girl sits on my bookshelf as a reminder that sometimes the only solution is distance.'

And then there's the Grand Canyon. Swarms of tourists disembark from trains or park their cars at odd angles. Backpackers double-check their water; photographers study the angle of the sun. All hubbub ceases at the majestic and ancient rim. The geologic erosion reveals strata and time, history so overwhelming that many visitors don't consider trying to comprehend it, but buy postcards instead.

The hike to Hermit's Rest amid boulders, juniper and mesquite brings me closer to the life of the canyon. It looks serene, but I know as I snap Hula Girl's picture it's an illusion. The river runs swift to taps in LA; ravens soar for pleasure; two condors tend their eggs; cacti, wildflowers and shrubs are in bloom. Nature is busy, ongoing, and greater than I am. I zip Hula Girl into the pocket of my backpack, with the reminder to take it all in and enjoy.

TIP!

For inspiration, watch the hit French comedy *Amélie* (2001), directed by Jean-Pierre Jeunet and starring the delightfully impish Audrey Tautou and the dishy Mathieu Kassovitz. Be sure to pay close attention to the activities of a certain travelling garden gnome.

MONOPOLY · TRAVEL

HYPOTHESIS:	Explore a city by using the Monopoly board as a map.
APPARATUS:	A Monopoly board to your chosen city, a pair of dice, tokens etc.
	Note: some aficionados like to play this game 'live', using mobile phones to communicate positions to other players.
METHOD:	Visit the streets, stations, jail, car park, water and electricity companies of your chosen city by throwing the dice and following the official rules of the game.

INTRODUCTORY NOTES:

Ironically, Monopoly[1] was invented by a poor, unemployed man, Charles B. Darrow of Pennsylvania, during the Depression in 1934. Today the game is licensed to more than 45 countries and appears in 26 different languages. According to the official website, the longest game in history took 70 days to complete. The silliest, longest Monopoly games ever played took 99 hours (in a bathtub), 45 days (underwater) and upside down (36 hours). Shamelessly capitalistic, Monopoly is a game where it is only possible to win at another's expense; winners live it up in Mayfair, while the losers tough it out on Old Kent Road.

A number of societies have sprung up devoted to the playing of live Monopoly, but this experiment can also be played alone or with friends. Players of this game are advised to take a 'Get out of Jail Free' card with them, choose their tokens carefully, and be aware that Free Parking may be in short supply.

1. Monopoly® is a registered trademark of Hasbro, Inc. The Monopoly Travel concept is not endorsed by or associated with Hasbro.

S plit in two during the Cold War between capitalist West Berlin and Communist East Berlin, Germany's capital was deprived of Monopoly until its reunification in 1990 – though there may have been several clandestine versions in black market circulation, all carefully hand-coloured. The official version, now found in every toy shop, follows an urban trajectory that begins in blue-collar Lützowplatz and ends in the ostentatious Ku'damm and Unter den Linden – an entire visitor's itinerary.

The shop where we buy our game is also our point of departure. We rid ourselves of unnecessary baggage by dumping the plastic green houses and red hotels on the footpath, as well as the 'Chance' and 'Community Chest' cards, so that all that is left to do is to throw the dice. Three and five make eight: Kollwitzplatz. Tally-ho!

First note to self: it's no mean feat navigating one's way about town using only a Monopoly board. The Berliners are as helpful as can be, but they are evidently more used to providing directions to out-of-towners with the assistance of a more conventional city map. They smile as they pass by, rarely stopping to indicate with a wave of the hand the general direction in which we should be heading. It takes us the better part of an hour to find Kollwitzplatz, the Aladdin's Cave of the intelligentsia under the Communist regime, and since transformed into Berlin's boho mecca, replete with design-heavy cafés, art galleries and deluxe squats.

One and six: Bahnhof Zoo, where you can find practically anything: showers, newspapers from all over the world, Italian-style espresso, poppyseed bagels and a troupe of Berlin dancers shoehorned into extravagant costumes.

'We rid ourselves of unnecessary baggage by dumping the plastic green houses and red hotels on the footpath.'

Six and three: Alexanderplatz, that paragon of Soviet-era architecture. The statue of Karl Marx still stands. Fly-by-night hawkers have a range of appropriately themed products on offer: T-shirts, caps, mugs, disposable lighters, snow domes and G-strings bearing the likeness of the father of Communism.

Two ones: Olympischestrasse. Its proximity to Alexanderplatz on the board should not be taken for geographical neighbourliness. The peaceful avenue, lined with chichi villas and leading to the old Nazi

Olympic stadium, is in fact 20km from Alexanderplatz.

Four and two: Go to jail. Do not pass 'Go'. Tegel prison has no visiting hours. The high concrete walls, watchtowers, barbed wire and surveillance cameras dissuade us from attempting to bribe the guards with our thick wads of 10,000 and 50,000 Monopoly Deutschmarks.

The random throws of the dice take us fleetingly through diverse landscapes: from Orianenstrasse, a throwback to suburban Istanbul, to the futuristic glass cathedrals of Potsdamer Platz; from the housing estates of Friedrichstrasse to the Jugendstil mansions and fashion boutiques of Ku'damm.

In one weekend, we circumnavigate the board twice. We pass 'Go', but don't collect the 4000 Monopoly Deutschmarks stipulated in the rules of the game. At Checkpoint Charlie, however, a Berliner – intrigued by our modus operandi – invites us to sleep at her place in the bohemian neighbourhood of Kreuzberg, an invitation worth its weight in Community Chest cards. Our thanks, Andy.

DO NOT PASS GO...

Do Not Pass Go, written by the comedic British writer Tim Moore, charts the history of London through a systematic investigation of every stop on the Monopoly board. A longtime Monopoly devotee, Moore explains his childhood love for the game:

...*Monopoly* you could play from the end of the *Thunderbirds* until the start of *Doctor Who,* and wake up in the morning and play again, assembling and consuming hasty and inappropriate meals around the board and postponing trips to the lavatory until it was slightly too late. Because Monopoly made you feel important and grown up: managing money, doing deals, getting arrested. It was a fight to the death, a game that was all about forcing your family and friends ever so slowly down onto their knees before mercilessly punting them into the gutter. And, best of all, those were real gutters, on real streets, a real city.[1]

1. From *Do Not Pass Go: From the Old Kent Road to Mayfair* by Tim Moore, published by Yellow Jersey. Reprinted by permission of The Random House Group Ltd and AP Watt Ltd on behalf of Tim Moore.

Nostalgia Trip

HYPOTHESIS:	Indulge (or relieve) your nostalgia for a place once visited by seeking it out in your own home town.
APPARATUS:	A sense of nostalgia or homesickness; a map or guidebook may also be useful.
METHOD:	1) Decide where you'd like to be and what you'd like to be doing (eg eating *kimchi* in Seoul, dancing the tango in Buenos Aires, hiking in Ecuador), then try to do it in your home town.
	Or
	2) Apply a foreign map or guidebook to your own town, choose a destination (eg the art gallery), see what you find there and compare it with the description in your guidebook. (If streets etc don't match perfectly, improvise.)

INTRODUCTORY NOTES:

While Nostalgia Trip can be used to evoke the memories of yesteryear, it could also serve as a substitute for the real thing.

In *The Art of Travel,* by contemporary philosopher Alain de Botton, the author recounts an episode from J. K. Huysman's novel *À Rebours* (1884), in which the central character, the travel-phobic Duc des Esseintes, is inspired to travel to London following a morning's reading of Dickens. Packed, suitably attired and ready to go, he awaits the next train from Paris to London. While he does so he kills some time, purchasing – and reading – Baedeker's *Guide to London* from an English bookshop and enjoying a drink in a wine bar frequented by English expats, before going to an English tavern where he samples a typically British meal of oxtail soup, smoked haddock, roast beef and potatoes, topped off with a few pints of ale and a piece of Stilton. When the time comes for him to leave for London, des Esseintes changes his mind: having enjoyed the 'Englishness' of his experience to the fullest, he fears the real thing will only disappoint. He returns home, never to leave it again.

LABORATORY RESULTS 1

**Courtesy of Experimental
Tourist Carmen Michael,
Sydney, Australia.**

☙

I once went to Rio for a one-week holiday but stumbled into a ring of Brazilian bohemians and didn't resurface until six months later, when the police apologetically explained that I had outstayed my visa. As I touched down in Sydney, my imagination was still drowning in Brazil's lush jungles, hypnotic sambas and the zest of its extraordinary people.

Now, some time later, I'm sitting in a bar, looking for Rio in the unlikely location of George St, Sydney. I down a poorly made *caiparinha* in which the essential *cachaça* (sugar-cane whisky) has been sacrilegiously replaced with Bacardi rum, and talk to Rosina, a Brazilian living in Sydney. She tells me that the place to find Rio in Sydney is Bondi. Bondi!? Having lived there half my life, it didn't exactly fit my image of bohemian Rio…

Nonetheless, on a Saturday morning as I pass under the crumbling arches of the Bondi Beach Pavilion (our own little version of Rio's magnificent Lapa arches) and look down on all the sun-tanning hedonists below, the differences between Rio and Sydney shrink to the size of a G-string bikini. I meet up with Marielu, an instructor of the Brazilian martial art dance *capoeira*, who now lives locally with a German Brazilophile who runs a Brazilian music radio show. I join her class in a room at the beach pavilion, which shares the space with an energetic woman teaching samba dancing. But the combination of jet lag (poor fitness levels), change of diet (a belly full of bad rum) and culture shock (the rigours of *capoeira* cartwheels) induce a state of nausea, and I shamefully throw up.

'The combination of jet lag (poor fitness levels), change of diet (a belly full of bad rum) and culture shock (the rigours of capoeira cartwheels) induce a state of nausea.'

Still feeling green and sweating *caiparinhas*, I decide to take the immersion process a little more gently. I wander around the pavilion, past the card players sitting as immoveable as their stone tables, and catch a drifting twang of the Brazilian *berimbou*. The lonely player is Walter, an Italian-Australian who organises Sydney's very own Escola da Samba.

And thus begins a weekend that fast becomes a blur of Brazilian travellers, musicians, dancers and students. I meet the thrice-divorced and dramatic Syzi, the seductive Sergio from Recife and a flirtatious backpacker from São Paulo. I am invited to the Brazilian national day in Marrickville, a gig by the big band sound of Son Veneno and a rehearsal for Escola da Samba. I visit the Gloria Café in Petersham, where I lounge alongside huddles of Portuguese men staving off their hunger and nostalgia with red wine, cigarettes and *feijoada*, the mother dish of the famed Brazilian version. Later, at home, I listen to Marielu's husband's radio programme and let the honeyed voices of bossa nova drift into my dreams.

There was no *cavaquino*, no old men playing drums on the pavement and, alas, no tight Lycra stretched inconceivably over huge asses, but I did meet the eclectic and elusive Brazilian tribe of Sydney. I had expected to discover new areas of Sydney but ended up fine-combing my own backyard – now I can only guess at how many other layers of the city are visible to the eye of a traveller rather than that of an indifferent local.

It's early evening in Helsinki, and the sun is sinking low in the sky. I'm walking home from work, and as I glance left and right to cross the street I suddenly have an eerie feeling of being not in the present moment but somewhere else. I take a second look to the right. A huge, dark mountain overlooks the city, and I immediately recognise its form: Jabal Nuqum, just east of San'a, the capital of Yemen.

There are no mountains in southern Finland, but the shady cloud with the mountain shape that hovers over the city is featureless, like Nuqum obscured by dust...

I first visited Yemen 20 years ago, and immediately fell in love with the country. I have kept returning there ever since, travelling, meeting people, snapping photos, learning the language, writing a guidebook. Anything can trigger my nostalgia. What I miss most is the diversity, for nothing in Yemen is like Finland, where I live. Yemen is a small country that has it all: mountains, deserts, beaches, tropical and arid climates, bustling cities in the grip of modernisation, ancient ruins and an age-old tribal culture.

When I reach home I realise just how badly I long for San'a. I ask my wife where she would like to be if we were in San'a right now. She mentions a modest 1st-floor teahouse overlooking the busy Bab al-Yaman square. I fetch our tattered tourist map of San'a from the bookshelf. 'We're here now, in the Manakha hotel', I say. 'Let's go for a walk and find the teahouse.' She catches the idea immediately.

We head out the front door and orientate ourselves. Nuqum is nowhere to be seen, and the sky is now clear.

At the next block we find ourselves facing Hietalahti Square, marked as Tahrir Square on the map. We seem somehow to be on the wrong side of it, so we take corrective action and proceed two blocks along the square's southern side. Oddly, the theatre at the eastern end of the square is not marked on the map, despite its 100-year-old appearance.

'Nothing in Yemen is like Finland, where I live.'

Next we turn right to walk seven blocks along Ali Abdul Moghni St, hilariously renamed al-Bertinkatu. Well, the Yemenis do have a habit of changing street names every few blocks!

The map has no names for the crossing streets, so we count them instead. After six blocks we arrive at a park, missing from our map, but the street continues as a tree-lined avenue anyway. 'Don't those poplars look like eucalypts?' My wife doesn't agree.

Next we encounter a major street. No street sign is visible but we regain

confidence in our map reading, as this must be Zubayri St. We continue left and don't bother to count blocks any more. After half a kilometre we should cross the seasonal river, Sa'ila, and see the old city wall on our left-hand side. We arrive and find there is no bridge over a dry riverbed, but a wall still stands. The old mud-brick wall must have collapsed, however, as a modern steel construction is now built around the premises of what the map says should be the Russian embassy.

At the end of the street, instead of the bustling Bab al-Yaman square and charming teahouse we find the Eteläsatama ferry terminal and its Tuuliviiri Restaurant. The ferry is about to leave, and the place is teeming with visitors from Stockholm. Nobody drinks tea here. We decide to blend in with the crowd, and order two beers. Good-bye, San'a; hello Helsinki.

*

NOSTALGIA: IT'S NOT WHAT IT USED TO BE

Nostalgia for the 'good old days' is often the idealised and selective imagining of a mis-remembered past. When the Berlin Wall came tumbling down in 1989, the world was euphoric; the Cold War was finally over. But after the joyous reunification of Germany in 1990, reality settled in – like a hangover after a New Year's Eve Party. The economic wealth of the West failed to lift the former Socialist zone from its economic woes, social services were cut and resentments grew.

Some Easterners – or 'Ossies' as they are known in Germany – became disillusioned with the new regime. Nostalgia for the old days – or 'ostalgia'– was on the rise. This curious, bitter-sweet emotion is neatly realised in the cult film *Goodbye Lenin*. It tells the story of a son who goes to extraordinary lengths to prevent his mother from learning that the Berlin Wall has fallen. Having suffered a stroke on the night of the event, and having spent the ensuring months in a coma, she must be protected from further shocks. The film was directed by Wolfgang Becker in 2003, and demonstrates how memories evolve with the passing of time.

OPUS TOURISTICUS

HYPOTHESIS: Undertake a journey inspired by a work of literature, art, cinema or music.

APPARATUS: A list of inspiring works of art with suitably far-flung titles.

METHOD: Compile a list of literature, art, music or cinema with a travel theme. For example, *A Passage to India, The Burghers of Calais,* 'One Night in Bangkok' and *Leningrad Cowboys go America.* The title will ideally contain a specific location, but it doesn't have to; for instance, Serge Gainsbourg's cult pop tune 'Sea, Sex and Sun' is presumably evocative enough to inspire some interesting adventures.

INTRODUCTORY NOTES:

Opus Touristicus was first tested by Latourex as 'new wave tourism' (a tongue-in-cheek prod at New Wave Cinema). It was inspired by *Last Year in Marienbad*, the legendary film by Alain Resnais and Alain Robbe-Grillet, and by the works of Jean-Luc Godard (*Breathless*) and François Truffaut (*The 400 Blows*).

Be warned that travels inspired by these films could involve meaningless sequences with matchboxes, enigmatic silences, cute French women and lots of cigarettes.[1] Choose carefully: Pink Floyd's *Dark Side of the Moon* could prove expensive; Alex Garland's *The Beach* might seem a safe bet but could degenerate into something closer to *Lord of the Flies;* and Marcel Proust's six volumes of *In Search of Lost Time* is probably best suited to retirees.

Note: Opus Touristicus en masse can have unintended consequences. For instance, Peter Mayle's *A Year in Provence* has led to marmalade and English breakfast tea rivalling coffee and croissants in popularity in some parts of France.

Preliminary reading (optional)

Some titles may elicit a variety of interpretations; for example, 'Norwegian Wood' evokes a Beatles song, a novel by Japanese author Haruki Murakami and, in the story that follows, a Norwegian folk tale:[2]

Once upon a time there was a wayward, wilful princess who always had to have the last word. One day her father, the king, makes a promise that whoever can make her hold her tongue will win the princess and half the kingdom.

One day three brothers decide to try their luck. Along the way, the youngest brother, named Ash Lad, finds a dead magpie. 'Look what I found!' he yells. 'Put it down. What are you going to do with that?' asks the eldest brother. 'Oh, I've got nothing better to do, and nothing better to carry, so I'll just take it along with me,' Ash Lad replies gaily. As their journey continues, Ash Lad repeats the routine with a broken saucer, the worn-out sole of a shoe, and so on.

When they arrive at the castle the two eldest brothers try to out-talk the princess, but fail. Finally it's Ash Lad's turn, who matches the princess using the objects he has found on his way. 'You're bent on wearing me out, aren't you?' says the princess finally. 'No, you're not worn out, but this is!' says Ash Lad, holding up the worn-out sole. The princess, short of a comeback line, has to hold her tongue and Ash Lad wins both the girl and half the kingdom.

---

1. Film buffs may prefer to describe these sequences as 'laden with deep, symbolic meaning'. **2.** This account is modelled on 'The Princess Who Always Had to Have the Last Word', one of Norway's most famous folk tales, summarised by Bente Jensen. For the original translation, see *Norwegian Folk Tales: From the Collection of Peter Christen Asbjørnsen and Jørgen Moe*, translated by Pat Shaw and Carl Norman (Oslo: Dreyers Forlag, 1994).

LABORATORY RESULTS 1

'Norwegian Wood', Courtesy of Experimental Tourist Bente Jensen, Tromsø, Norway.

✿

I like this folk tale (see Preliminary Reading, earlier) about the Norwegian wood because it says a lot about people and their values. This folktale shows that even if something looks like rubbish it can be gold if you use your imagination. It also suggests that if you don't judge things by their appearances you will find true happiness – and perhaps even the love of your life.

So, like our hero Ash Lad, I decide to try my luck in the Norwegian wood to see if I can win a prince and half the kingdom.

But while garbage and dead animals littered Ash Lad's world, the modern Norwegian wood seems comparatively spotless. After a short walk I find my first item: a Jehovah's Witness flyer. A voice in my head nags me, saying, 'Put it down. What are you going to do with that?' But I calmly reply with a loud voice (like any good Ash Lad would), 'Oh, I've got nothing better to do, and nothing better to carry, so I'll just take it along with me.'

Two boys, who are chasing each other with sticks nearby, stop and ogle me curiously and snigger, before running away. Further down the road I find two yellow candles in the moss. I put them in my bag. 'Put them down. What are you going to do with that?' the voice in my head whispers. 'Oh, I've got nothing better to do, and nothing better to carry, so I'll just take them along with me,' I answer, a bit softer this time so nobody will hear me.

Despite my keen eye I find no dead animals that may come in handy as a meal afterwards. I can, however, spot a living crow, that is sitting in a treetop. But when I climb up to catch it, it flies away, heckling me with a '*kra kra kra*'. When I climb down again and fall on the melted snow, I discover a final item: a blue and white and very wet mitten. 'Look what I found! Look what I found!' I yell. But not even the stick-chasing boys can hear me now.

With my Jehovah's Witness' flyer, my candles and my mitten I am now ready for my prince and the world. I wait by the side of the road for someone to come by (there aren't many princes around these days, so a stranger will have to do). Perhaps he is interested in a candle-lit dinner (where did that crow go?) or maybe he'd like to discover God's kingdom on earth? (Check flyer reading: 'Why should you read the Bible? You will understand why there are so many problems in the world...') If I tell him I have a secret surprise for him (a mitten), he will come with me for sure. Because even modern folk tales have a happy ending, right?

᪥

LABORATORY RESULTS 2

A Room with a View, Courtesy of Experimental Tourist Trent Van der Werf, Europe.

᪥

Hotel Voorstraat, Dordrecht, Holland
Hotel Voorstraat is draped in the shadow of the imposing Grote Kerk, home to the largest bells in the region, which conveniently sound morbid Gothic parlour music on the hour, half-hour and quarter-hour...

A room with a view is important: just ask Helena Bonham Carter. Well, her character in the Merchant Ivory adaptation of E.M. Forster's book, anyway. So when I finally had the opportunity to travel through Europe I decided to follow in her footsteps. I wanted a room. And I wanted a view. Or at least a window.

Thankfully, all of the rooms I stayed in had a window, and most opened onto the outdoors rather than a communal laundry. This was vital, as I was to embark upon a trip where, using the book's title as a starting point, I would rigorously document in photographs the views from my accommodation, whatever they might be. I planned to absent myself from the happy-snap trail and reveal the truth: a unique visual insight into each of my destinations, without the iconic monuments.

Of course there's no singular truth, but there is infinite variety. Acknowledging the everyday surroundings that exist accessibly, and abundantly, in every tourist mecca was rewarding. My exploration of the apparently mundane forced me to observe less like a tourist, and more like an interested third party. My images didn't turn out to be painterly panoramas dissected by the river Arno, but then I didn't visit Florence in the springtime.

Casa Maria, Rua 25 de Abril, Lagos, Portugal
Visibly unimpressed by the luxurious scale
of Portuguese teacups, a rare expanse of
cobblestones is startling between the tourists
en route to the nearest British-themed pub.

Best Hostel, Pest, Budapest, Hungary
From the grim filth of the infuriatingly named
Best Hostel, a vista of life-endangering
dedication to cleanliness is simply heart
warming.

Kabul, Plaça Reial, Barcelona, Spain
A resident of perpetually rowdy Plaça Reial
feigns interest as the emergency services,
stoned tourists and street performers converge
to observe a house on fire.

Chez Naomi, Villeneuve-la-Garenne, France
An enthusiastic double-tribute to the Eiffel
Tower, and a Pompidou Centre–inspired
lifestyle development grace the suburban
skyline afforded by Chez Naomi.

Obscure pensão, Lisbon, Portugal
Converted to offices, the well-proportioned
building opposite my *pensão* offered cheery
photocopying action all day from 10am – perfect
for the work-sick corporate traveller on a budget.

red carnation crusade

HYPOTHESIS: Discover a city with a group of strangers all wearing an easily identifiable token.

APPARATUS: Internet access, a cunning plan, a liking for red carnations, charisma!

Note: red carnations can be exchanged for any other common denominator: red hats, Viking helmets, ballet tutus, safety glasses etc.

METHOD: Post a notice on an Internet travel forum requesting a rendezvous with travellers at a certain time and place. Nominate an activity to undertake as a group, eg pulling faces at the guards at Buckingham Palace, tap-dancing down the Champs-Élysées etc. Ask everyone to wear the same easily identifiable token. Consider taking a photograph of yourself with your fellow travellers and try to recruit new members as you go.

INTRODUCTORY NOTES:

When trying to attract a crowd it's a good idea to offer a novel experience or promote a higher ideal to potential recruits. For a historical example, study *Monkey* by Wu Cheng-en,[1] an adaptation of which was made into a kooky cult TV series in the 1970s. It tells the tale of the quietly charismatic priest Tripitaka, who convinces a mischievous Monkey, the slothful Pigsy, a moody antisocial fish named Sandy and a dragon (aka 'horse') to join him on a quest to take the Buddhist scrolls from China to India and back. In a more recent but no less challenging example, the American photographer Spencer Tunick has drawn crowds of thousands with the promise of mass nudity in the name of art.[2]

Red Carnation Crusade is a novel way to experience one of the greatest things about travel: meeting new people from all walks of life. It gives you the opportunity to inspire not only yourself but others – plus you could develop your own cult following. Tripitaka and his friends not only survived 81 adventures, they also ended up with VIP passes to Heaven.

1. *Monkey* is the partial translation of the great 16th-century Chinese novel *Journey to the West*. **2.** You can find out about forthcoming mass nude photo shoots and sign up to take part at www.spencertunick .com. Examples of Tunick's work can be viewed at www.nakedworlddoc.com, a site dedicated to a documentary that follows the showy but somewhat abrasive Tunick and his long-suffering photographic assistant John around the world.

'If there were any questions about our laboratory, I believe they have now been answered: New York is definitely the world's salad bowl.'

'You look like the Tin Man,' cackles a crazy old lady with a toothless grin. Admittedly, my appearance is pretty comical: I have placed an aluminum deflector beanie on my head while I wait to meet my as-yet unidentified group of co-travelers. All in the name of Experimental Travel. At least this is what I tell myself before I begin to believe that I too should be chasing the pigeons into the fountain.

Other than the peculiar toothless old woman, who apparently is above placing tinfoil on her own head to participate in my experiment, no-one even gives me a passing glance. Such is life in New York City, where on any given day you can meet three people claiming to be a member of the Holy Trinity having a beer in Hell's Kitchen.

Yet this zaniness also makes the Big Apple the perfect laboratory to perfect my experiment in travel: assembling a group of strangers via an electronic medium to meet wearing the same article of identifying clothing.

For today's mission, strangers domed in tinfoil have agreed to rendezvous at City Hall. Once assembled, the group will proceed down Broadway to 'storm' the city's famous monument to capitalism: the Wall Street Bull. Predictably, this particular casting call was met with much trepidation. Reactions on the larger Internet travel boards ranged from the ubiquitous 'that is so passé' to the 'you must be up to something illegal', while others wondered if I was the second coming of Spencer Tunick.

To their dismay no laws are to be broken, and no animals harmed; all that is needed is a brave group of people with an affinity for tinfoil headgear. In a city of eight million inhabitants, I am here to tell you there are exactly three people who share such an affliction: me, and two random females who have nothing better to do on a beautiful April day.

Once the group is amassed, and pleasantries exchanged, we set off on our quest. Our saunter is filled with exchanges of life stories and is, as it turns out, a unifying experience. I suppose this is the natural progression of walking down the main drag with aluminum foil on your head.

After 15 minutes our target is in sight. We have arrived at the core of capitalism's lie, thronged with camera-touting out-of-towners, ice-cream salesmen and gray-market dealers hawking fake Rolexes and pirated DVDs. One of the native New York ladies who has joined me has no time for the nonsense of tourism that has befallen 'our' Bull and immediately proclaims that she will have her picture taken next and that we need volunteers!

Not surprisingly, given the well-documented history of mob mentality, once the multitude see how much fun the three tinfoil-wearing whackos are having, other madcap fools soon have no trouble posing with foil on their head for a photo session. And like the city itself, our multicultural final group is made up of a German expat who now calls the United States home, a lost tourist whose next stop is to enquire about purchasing the Brooklyn Bridge, and three children who between them speak a total of three different words of English. If there were any questions about our laboratory, I believe they have now been answered: New York is definitely the world's salad bowl.

SNOWBALL EFFECT

If you're not up for recruiting strangers, why not test the snowball effect with a bunch of friends? Here's how to do it:

Take a walk around the city and stop by a friend's house (friend A). Ask them to join you and continue on your walk to visit friend B. Collect friend B and take them to friend C's house, then entice them to accompany you all to friend D's house and so on until you are a large group and are too knackered to walk any further. When you've gathered together as many friends as you can, why not find a small place (eg a cloakroom, sandwich shop, cupboard or bathroom) to squeeze into for a game of sardines?

Rent a Tourist

HYPOTHESIS: Explore the working life of the city and learn about the locals by renting yourself out to help with daily chores.

APPARATUS: Paints or pens to make a sign, a sales pitch and a device to draw attention to yourself (eg loudspeaker, red flashing light).

METHOD: Stand in the main square or plaza with a sign advertising yourself as a tourist 'for rent'. If you have time, consider handing out a flyer that lists your possible duties. Avoid dark alleys, backstreets etc which could lead to confusion over your, ahem, 'job description'.

INTRODUCTORY NOTES:

In 2003 the self-called White Group, comprising more than 30 academics working in the fields of design, technology and tourism, met in Rome to explore alternative modes of travel and the interaction between tourists and locals. 'Inspired by Situationist-like explorations of the absurd and sociological "breaching experiments",[1] we played in and with the city in order to design something playful for the people in it.'[2]

The idea was to transform travellers from 'bovine hordes' of gaping tourists into 'urban players', where meaningful and unpredictable interaction could occur. Three 'design' models[3] were trialled, one of them being 'Rent a Tourist', an experiment that proved unsuccessful in Rome but was a hit for us in India.

1. Pioneered by Harold Garfinkel, 'breaching experiments' were popular with sociologists during the 1960s. The idea was to identify and test social norms by purposefully behaving inappropriately. Give these a try: Step into a lift. Rather than turning around to face the door, face your fellow passengers. Make eye contact. Or, behave like a guest in your own home: eg ring the doorbell, ask questions like 'May I sit down?' and 'Could I have a glass of water?', and see whether polite guest behaviour is considered 'polite' at home. **2.** A. Galloway, M. Ludvigsen, H. Sundholm and A. Munro, 'From Bovine Horde to Urban Players: Multidisciplinary Interaction Design for Alternative City Tourisms', a workshop position paper for Mobile and Ubiquitous Multimedia (MUM), 10–12 December 2003, Norrköping, Sweden. **3** The other models were a 'tour T-shirt' and a high-tech, dice-like 'cube', both to be used to design travel itineraries; see www.purselipsquarejaw.org/index.php.

LABORATORY RESULTS

Courtesy of Experimental Tourist Steven Baker, Hampi, India.

T he place: Hampi, southern India. The time: midday. The temperature: around 42°C in the shade. As I started my search for work in the somewhat shade-free zone of Hampi's main bazaar, the words 'Englishmen' and 'mad dogs' sprang to mind. It was bad enough that *I* thought I was crazy, but Shiva knows what the locals were thinking as they witnessed this tambourine-banging, sandwich-board–clad figure proclaiming 'Rent a tourist! Rent a tourist!' every 10 paces. I had earlier decided that a sign offering myself for hire in big letters against a backdrop of Hindu gods, with my head superimposed onto a picture of Krishna with a cow, would be a tasteful yet subtle method of advertising. Just to make sure the point was clear to all, the text was printed in English, Hindi and the state language, Kannada.

I was delirious with sun when sometime later I found myself accepting the position of waiter from an overworked restaurant owner. The next hour passed in a blur of *chai* and chapatis as I dealt with the lunch-time rush, and it was with a sense of triumph that I emerged from the restaurant with a crisp 10-rupee note in my hand.

Word soon spread of the bizarre, bazaar 'Rent a Tourist'. Five hours and five jobs later I was able to add not just waiter but English teacher, street vendor/children's entertainer, road sweeper and rickshaw driver to my CV.

Just as I was contemplating early retirement, an official-looking, flag-waving vehicle pulled up, and I was promptly hired by a local politician to canvass for the forthcoming Indian elections. Alas, my brief foray into politics didn't prove to be as lucrative as I had hoped; after much leaflet-delivery legwork, the right honourable gentleman sped off into a sunset of flags and dust. And, er, the small matter of payment? Gone the way of many a politician's promise...

Finally, heading back to my guesthouse after a long day and with less than 50 rupees in my pocket, I unexpectedly secured my last gig, and it was here that I really made my millions. I discovered that in the dry temple town that is Hampi, a barman surreptitiously serving 'special' drinks to travellers from an innocuous teashop could make some very serious money. Bemused and confounded in equal measures by the placard around my neck, the clientele of increasingly inebriated backpackers tipped rather well. No doubt they thought I had become one of those poor lost tourists who had spent all of their money in India and was now desperately saving for a passage home.

The next morning I counted out just over 98 rupees[4] in used notes and small change, and handed over my hard-earned wages, and rather ill-gotten gains, to the local temple.

4. Equivalent to around £1 or US$2

BYOA

Why sit back and wait for the town to entertain you when you can entertain the town by playing Bring Your Own Attraction? Set up shop on a makeshift table or blanket in the main square and put on a bit of a show. Given that luggage space is likely to be an issue, recommended BYOAs could include a mini-expo of pet rocks or an old-fashioned flea circus. For inspiration, you might like to check out *Portable Museum (Boîte-en-valise)* by the artist Marcel Duchamp, who was associated with both the Surrealist and Dadaist movements. Starting in 1936, Duchamp made seven versions of a portable museum containing tiny replicas of his most famous works, including *Fountain*, *The Large Glass* and *Nude Descending a Staircase*. Alternatively, declare yourself an ambassador for your country and conduct impromptu Q&A sessions with interested passers-by.

HYPOTHESIS: See how far your thumb will take you.

APPARATUS: A large piece of card (approximately 20cm x 50cm), a thick black pen and a destination.

METHOD: Go to your nearest motorway (or similar) with a backpack and a large piece of card. Write the name of a faraway destination on your sign, eg Buenos Aires, Shanghai, Timbuktu, Humpty Doo. Avoid excessive detail (Flat 7, 255 Northolm Rd, down the road from the post office, Essex, UK) Stand by the side of the road, stick your thumb out and wait...

Note: if travelling internationally, be sure to research the local hitchhiking signal – standing with your thumb out is not universally understood.

INTRODUCTORY NOTES:

For the impoverished 'Okies' depicted in John Steinbeck's *Grapes of Wrath,* hitchhiking was the only way to travel across the US during the Great Depression of the 1930s. While economic necessity has always been a motivator for hitchhiking, over time it also came to signify alternative lifestyle choices. During the 1950s, hitchhiking was the preferred method of transport for beat writers such as Jack Kerouac, Allen Ginsberg and William S. Burroughs, who preferred to spend their money on drugs, alcohol and typewriting tape rather than on mundane expenses like transport. During the 1970s hitchhiking became synonymous with freewheeling hippie travellers and the search for personal freedom. Today hitchhiking may be considered an ecological choice for those keen to save on fossil fuels, but it has largely declined in popularity thanks to increased awareness of the associated dangers and the introduction of legislation to curb the practice. Nonetheless, die-hard hitchhikers are still out there. In 1994 Alexey Vorov, president of the St Petersburg Autostop League (PASL), hitchhiked around the world by plane, boat and car. For details of international hitchhiking competitions (conducted in pairs), check out hitchhiking clubs such as the Lithuanian-based Vilnius Hitchhiking Club (www.autostop.lt).

Slight-Hitch Travel is just like regular hitchhiking, except that you're trying to get a hell of a lot further. Whether you manage to get a lift from, say, Florence (Italy) to Cape Town (South Africa), is uncertain, but what is certain is that you'll have an interesting journey along the way. Should you get picked up, Slight-Hitch Travel is a sure-fire conversation starter.

Note: obviously hitchhiking, slight or otherwise, can be a risky undertaking, so think carefully before undertaking this experiment. It's recommended that you travel with at least one friend.

LABORATORY RESULTS
Courtesy of Experimental Tourist Jeremy Moon, Los Angeles, USA.

Part One: Santa Monica Freeway, Los Angeles

I've only just found a suitable spot by the side of the freeway, put down my pack and pulled out my 'SYDNEY' sign, when the local police pull up to let me know that it isn't safe to hitch-hike around here and that there are laws against it. I decide the best way to stay out of trouble is to be as Aussie ocker as I can, and explain what I am doing. I put on my best Steve Irwin accent (I wish I was wearing khaki shorts) and say, 'Crikey mate, are you fair dinkum?'

The officer laughs and asks me where I am from.

'Way down under,' I deadpan. 'We don't have cities like this back home!'

Realising I'm harmless, he kindly proceeds to tell me at length about the local bus system, and recommends the best sights to see in his city. Then he asks me where I'm trying to get to, so I show him my sign again. 'Sydney, Oztralia? You'll have to take a plane,' he says. (No kidding, I think.) Taking a deep breath he begins, 'The best way to get to the airport is…'

Part Two: Teotihuacan, Mexico

I've been standing in the hot sun with my thumb out for about 20 minutes and I'm starting to wish I never even considered trying something this silly. All I want is to get to *somewhere* – anywhere but by the side of this highway. My sign says 'SYDNEY' but I'll be happy to go any place that has shade or cold beer (preferably both).

Every car that zooms past is full of evil, selfish people who should be

taking pity on me. I'm in a country where I don't speak the language and I'm trying to hitchhike to a city that's on another continent. Sure, I wouldn't pull over to pick up a person who is so obviously insane, but one of these cars must be carrying a more friendly soul.

Great! A bus is slowing down – maybe it will stop? No, the tourists on board just wanted to take photos of the idiot on the side of the road... Hang on, that nice green van is stopping. I'm so happy I don't even notice it's full of people in green uniforms all holding large guns.

> **'A bus is slowing down – maybe it will stop? No, the tourists on board just wanted to take photos of the idiot on the side of the road...'**

'Don't you know that hitchhiking in this country is a shootable offence?' yells one of the soldiers. (Remember, I don't speak the local language, so I'm really just guessing that's what he is yelling at me). But I actually do understand a word from the next sentence he shouts at me. *'Identificación!'* comes out loud and clear.

As I dig out my passport, I'm imagining that this guy has a trophy cabinet at home where he displays the passports of all the hapless hitchhikers he has shot. I hand over my passport and feel relief rush through me as he smiles and then laughs (I really should change that photo). He barks a command and

two of the soldiers jump down, grab my pack and fling it into the back of their truck, then proceed to do the same with me.

The truck pulls away and I fall to the floor. My pack slides towards the opening at the rear, trying to make a dash for freedom. My passport is still being passed around the soldiers, who are now either in hysterics or attempting to talk to me in English.

After about 30 minutes of bouncing and swerving around we grind to a halt and my pack and I are tossed out into the world again. Expecting the worst – a firing squad or a Mexican prison – I realise I've been dropped in front of Purisima station, on the outskirts of Mexico city.

The soldier with the loud voice gives me a wave and points towards the metro... A week later I leave for my next destination, Ireland. By plane.

HITCHHIKING WITH A FRIDGE

British comedian Tony Hawks enjoyed a journey with a difference when he hitchhiked around Ireland for a month with a smallish but highly inconvenient bar fridge – for a £100 bet. He later wrote a highly successful book about the experience called, not surprisingly, *Round Ireland with a Fridge*. Hitchhiking with large or absurd objects could have amusing results, but don't restrict yourself to white goods – why not try a goat, a double bass or a large, orange, wooden robot?

Hare

Slow-Return Travel

Tortoise

HYPOTHESIS: Experience the contrasting benefits and experiences of fast and slow methods of travel.

APPARATUS: A destination and access to fast and slow forms of transport. Fast forms of transport include space rockets, jet planes and high-tech Rollerblades. Slow forms include bicycles, moon boots (especially if worn while walking on sand) and stubborn animals such as donkeys and goats.

Note: speed is relative.

METHOD: Choose a faraway destination and travel there using the quickest form of transport you can find. For the return journey, do the reverse and choose transport that is as slow as possible.

INTRODUCTORY NOTES:

Marshall McLuhan was famous for his theories on media, but he also applied his revolutionary concept that 'the medium is the message' to transportation: 'The railway did not introduce movement or transportation or wheel or road into human society, but it accelerated and enlarged the scale of previous human functions, creating totally new kinds of cities and new kinds of work and leisure. This happened whether the railway functioned in a tropical or northern environment, and is quite independent of the freight or content of the railway medium.'[1]

McLuhan's argument is that the medium itself is the message because of the way in which it forms and shapes the message and its resulting impact on the individual and, by extension, on the whole of society. To take a simplistic example, imagine how you might experience Charles Dickens' *David Copperfield* in varied media; for instance, reading a vintage hardback, hearing it via a crackly radio broadcast or downloading it on the Internet – complete with cookies and hyperlinks.

Applying McLuhan's message to travel suggests that the form and relative speed of transportation *is* the journey itself. Thanks to air travel, we have become accustomed to arriving in a new place, experiencing new cultures and hearing new languages after a journey of just a few hours. Only a hundred years ago the same journey could have taken days, weeks or even months. All too often our aim while travelling is to get 'there' as fast as possible – but what happens to our travels when the medium is slow?

1. Marshall McLuhan, *Understanding Media* (New York: Signet Books, 1964).

Courtesy of Experimental
Tourists Mrs Joanna and Mr
Kevin Davison, Nepal.

We decided to incorporate the Slow-Return Travel experiment into a rafting trip in Nepal. The first stage of the journey took us from Pokhara to Baglung via bus, then we returned 'slowly' by taking a raft from Baglung, changing to another bus for the final stage of the journey from Kali Gandaki back to Pokhara.

FAST: Travelling in Nepal can be a long and arduous task, taking you up and down hills and valleys but covering little distance as the crow flies. The only quick form of transport in Nepal is by air, but being budget travellers this option is out of the question. Bus it is then. Nepal's bus drivers are on a par with their infamous South American counterparts, driving at breakneck speeds on dubious roads, with every other vehicle swerving desperately to avoid their path.

The 'fast' journey from Pokhara takes approximately five hours – only breaking for the Nepali staff to eat one of the numerous *dahl bhats* of the day. The bus offers us views of the landscape flashing by, mainly terraced farmland. People are going about their daily lives as we pass by, and our journey is interrupted only occasionally by the bother of passing through Nepal's numerous military checkpoints.

The ride itself is on a par with any Indian bus journey, and features frequent spine-shattering episodes and near misses from oncoming vehicles. I give the Nepali bus drivers credit for being able to keep the vehicles on those roads!

When we arrive at Baglung we have lunch and experience our first, but not last, encounter with abject poverty. The children from the nearby residence wait until we have finished dining so they can take back the remains of our lunch for their families to eat. It is a sad sight to see.

Our lunch over, the boats are assembled and loaded, and we receive our safety instructions before being let loose on the Kali Gandaki River.

SLOW: We spend the next three days rafting down the river through sequences of rapids and still water. The trip is amazing. The Kali Gandaki gorge is breathtaking, with the striking view of Annapurna a dramatic backdrop. Waterfalls cascade all around us, fish leap out of the water, and we are greeted by locals wherever we pass, from riverside to mountaintops. Eagles soar, kingfishers fish

and vultures lurk around in groups looking sinister.

The slow journey back to Pokhara gives us the opportunity to see aspects of Nepal that would be inaccessible by any other means of transport. But the real beauty is the absence of any noise except for that of nature. And that's something you just don't get when you travel at the speed of sound.

SYNCHRONISED TRAVEL

HYPOTHESIS: Travel a synchronised path with your friends and discover whether parallel lines ever meet.

APPARATUS: Two or more participants, a notebook and camera.

METHOD: Participants travel around their chosen locations using a 10-stage set of common directions, taking notes and photographs to record their experiences at each stage. Where directions don't match the environs, improvise.

1) The first stage is your starting point.

2) Walk in any direction for 50 to 100 paces, and then turn 180 degrees.

3) Continue walking in that direction until you see something blue.

4) Make a left turn and walk 50 to 70 paces.

5) Walk in any direction until you see something that either is or looks like the number 7 or 11.

6) Take the first left, and continue walking until you find somewhere to sit.

7) Choose any direction and walk for 25 to 50 paces.

8) Continue walking until you see an unusual colour, shape or texture. Turn 180 degrees.

9) Keep walking in any direction until you see an archway or an unusual architectural feature.

10) Head for home, but continue looking for something that catches your eye.

INTRODUCTORY NOTES:

Synchronised – or parallel – Travel enables you to see your own city with fresh eyes, without breaking your budget. It's also a very useful means of showing your city to friends from afar – or enjoying a holiday together, while apart! While this experiment includes photography, you don't have to take photos. Instead, you could do a dance, strike a pose, write a poem, enjoy a quiet moment or do nothing at all.

LABORATORY RESULTS

Courtesy of Experimental Tourists Bill and Ben, UK and Belgium.

We are old friends who now live in different countries. We used to travel together all over the place, but nowadays the finances aren't so good. We were looking for a way of going on holiday together, to somewhere we could both afford.

So we came up with Synchronised Travel. We decided to share our idea on Lonely Planet's Thorn Tree, and a dozen other folk said they'd like to join in. Coordinating a globally diverse experiment could be difficult, so we decided not to bother. Instead, we had a discussion and agreed on the 10 stages and a deadline for submitting individual results. At every stage, each participant was asked take a photo and make a note of their impressions. Cheating and rule-bending were permitted. Many people conducted their experiment in familiar surroundings, usually their home town, while others chose foreign destinations.

The participants found the experiment a fascinating experience, and most were surprised by just how much fun it was. 'I felt like I was seeing the place for the first time' was a common remark. By using arbitrary instructions as a guide, rather than tourist or local

(learned) expectations, people discovered new aspects of their environments, and gained new insights and appreciation for their chosen location.

The participants were all widely travelled, and recognised that travel can become routine and almost predictable. Participating in this experiment broke the model. It was exciting and interesting to look around a familiar place and discover new details, to actively search out interesting or unusual features, rather than the next item on a 'tourist shopping list'.

We were also keen to inspire participants' creative energies, to add an artistic element to their presentations. Participants were encouraged to use their imagination and all their senses to create something beyond a travelogue or journal. When they reported back after the experiment, participants noted that Synchronised Travel brought out their creative abilities.

The results from our experiment were put online (http://ttwt.knackered.net/travel/et/index.html), where they can be navigated by following an individual participant's journey or at random. As you can see, the whole is more than the sum of its parts.

BILL & BEN POEM

Bill and Ben are well-known entities on Lonely Planet's Thorn Tree travel forum. Enthusiastic and prolific contributors to the board since 1997, they were among the first to volunteer to participate in this Experimental Travel project, and quickly devised the travel experiment featured here. They also wrote a poem, sung to the tune of Cliff Richard's 'Summer Holiday', which we'd like to share with you:

We're all going on an experimental holiday
Joan Miró for a week or two
Eno and John Cage on our summer holiday
And more Dalí for me or you
For a week or two.
We're going where the sun shines darkly
We're going where the moon is blue
We've all seen it in the paintings
Now let's see if it's true.
Everybody has an experimental holiday
Doing things in obscurity
So we're going on an experimental holiday
To make our dreams come true
For me and you
For me and you.

1

The first stage is your starting point.

2

Walk in any direction for 50 to 100 paces, and then turn 180 degrees.

3

Continue walking in that direction until you see something blue.

4

Make a left turn and walk 50 to 70 paces.

5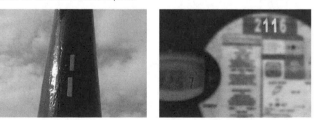

Walk in any direction until you see something that either is or looks like the number 7 or 11.

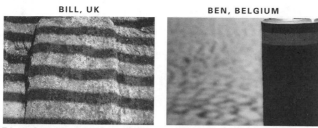

6

Take the first left, and continue walking until you find somewhere to sit.

7

Choose any direction and walk for 25 to 50 paces.

8

Continue walking until you see an unusual colour, shape or texture. Turn 180 degrees.

9

Keep walking in any direction until you see an archway or an unusual architectural feature.

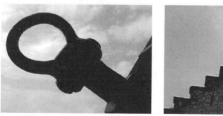

10

Head for home, but continue looking for something that catches your eye.

TAKING A LINE FOR A WALK allows you to 'graffiti'

Hypothesis:	Create an itinerary by drawing on a map.
Apparatus:	A map and a pencil.[1] You may also need transport, such as a bicycle or car.
Method:	Using a pencil or GPS device, superimpose a drawing on a map, which will then form your itinerary. You can draw anything you like, eg your name, a shape or something more complex. Your line can be as long or as short as you like.

1. High-tech toy fans may want to use a GPS device rather than a pencil.

the landscape without leaving a trace

INTRODUCTORY NOTES:

Paul Klee (1879–1940) was a Swiss painter and art theorist known for his whimsical, sometimes fantastical, paintings which were neither strictly abstract nor figurative. Klee's description of drawing as 'taking a line for a walk' provides the starting point for this particular experiment, which combines both art and movement. The title is also taken from an exhibition of GPS and 'foot doodles' that took place at X-Change Gallery in Oxford, UK, in 2002.

Taking a Line for a Walk allows you to 'graffiti' the landscape without leaving a trace. Your drawing may inform your travels (as it did for Don George; see p221) or it may operate independently of them. While you could conceivably do this experiment in your own neighbourhood, it also lends itself to longer distances.

For example, in 2002, as part of the exhibition at the X-Change Gallery, Hugh Pryor and Jeremy Wood decided to answer the question 'What's the world's biggest "IF"?' by drawing one of their own in southern England. Their 'IF' incorporated the aptly 'Iffy' destinations of Iffley, Iford, Ifield and Ifold. The resulting itinerary, which they 'drew' by car, was 863km long – the equivalent font size would be 319,334,400 points – and took a total of two days and six hours to complete. You can see the results of their experiment online at www .gpsdrawing.com/gallery/land/if.htm.

LABORATORY RESULTS 1
Courtesy of Experimental Tourist Don George, Piedmont, California, USA.

❀

Hearts and San Francisco go together. Tony Bennett. The Summer of Love. Poet George Sterling's 'cool, gray city of love'. And on the day of this experiment, heart sculptures decorate neighborhoods all over the city in a massive open-air exhibit.

So I take a red pen to a map of the city and trace a sloping heart shape any child would be proud of: my itinerary.

It's 11:50am on a sunny blue-sky day and I'm standing at the ferry building on San Francisco Bay. The salty smell of the sea wafts over the first lunch patrons sitting under canvas umbrellas at sidewalk restaurants. Two sleek men clink glasses of champagne. 'To San Francisco,' one says. 'To us', the other smiles.

> **'Two sleek men clink glasses of champagne. "To San Francisco", one says. "To us", the other smiles.'**

I cross under the balmy palms of the Embarcadero, but then encounter my first challenge: heart lines don't follow street lines. My itinerary plunges into an office building lobby, where I'm greeted by the clang of cymbals and boom-boom of drums and a Chinese dragon darting and leaping. A woman takes up a microphone: 'Welcome to the grand opening of the first exhibition at the new International Museum of Women. Today we celebrate women all over the world...'

Four blocks later the heart-line leads me to a corner I've passed dozens of times without ever noticing the statue of a young woman holding a baby, sculpted on a thick pedestal adorned with fishes, hula dancers, dogs and other figures. I circle the sculpture three times but can't find any plaque or notice – no title, no artist: a mystery.

Next I ascend a winding staircase to a packed outdoor restaurant at a hotel. I step inside, only to be swept into a swirling sea of blue suits, name tags and health products. A silky woman strokes my arm and smiles. 'Would you like to sample our latest skin enhancer?' She searches for my name tag. Security guards eye me to the men's room, where two name-tags are talking. Are you gonna do the deed tonight?' 'You bet I am – she gave me the green light!'

I walk briskly through the lobby and emerge into the sunlight. My heart-line leads me inexorably down a tight, garbage-scented alley where I squeeze past a parked SUV. Inside I glimpse long stockinged legs, a crumpled leopard-print dress and two torsos crushed in embrace: the SUV Lunch-time Motel. I duck through the service exit of a café and emerge opposite the Bureau of Citizenship and Immigration Services, where a shaven-headed monk in flowing brown robes and a young woman holding a baby, just like the statue I saw earlier, stand patiently in a long line.

My line leads to serene Walton Park, where a couple are sitting knee-to-knee in front of one of the city-wide heart sculptures, a big bronze piece. I walk over to see who made it – Jim Dine, 1984 – and hear: 'Do you want to go through with it or not?' 'That's what I'm saying – it's not an easy yes or no answer.' 'Then what is it?'

The trail beats on, past the metal-fenced tennis courts of the Golden Gateway Club, where a bright-yellow ball sails over the fence and bounces right into the delighted hands of a pink-dressed Asian girl walking with her mom. 'Love-forty,' a man shouts as the girl throws the ball into the air.

My itinerary ends at *Yin and Yang* by Robert Arneson, another work of art I've never seen before: two egg-shaped heads, one upright with an open mouth, talking; the other on its side, listening with one eye closed and a worried expression on its face.

I sit here for a long time and think about all the veins of yin and yang in the body of mankind. And in a patch of grass behind the Arneson, a man spreads a blanket for his lover, and their fingers intertwine: heart-lines.

LABORATORY RESULTS 2
Courtesy of Experimental Tourist Rachael Antony,
a World without Borders, Australia.

❧

A s the end of this Experimental Travel project drew near, I started to think about all those people who are free to travel, both near and far – experimentally or otherwise – and conversely, those who are not. As Australia's conservative government had recently been re-elected, my thoughts turned to asylum seekers and refugees who, having travelled so far and risked so much, were now languishing in Australian detention centres, cobbled by politics, bound in red tape, on the road to nowhere.

And then it occurred to me that I might make a small gesture against the status quo, an action that would be entirely pointless but might provide some personal relief. Using my car as a 'paintbrush' and the road as my 'canvas', I would take a line for a walk around a nearby immigration detention centre. Or, more specifically, using the power vested in me as a citizen of the world, I would cut through bureaucracy and with movement as my medium I would 'draw' a rubber stamp around the centre, in symbolic approval of the detainees' liberation into the free world.

I grabbed a map and charted my course. It turned out that my route reflected the history of immigration in Australia over the last 200 years. I would begin in the suburb of Collingwood, formerly home to Aboriginal groups such as the Wurundjeri people and now a bohemian district where the local indigenous people still hang out, but are most likely to be seen begging for small change. Heading down Victoria Parade (named after the empire-building British queen), I would pass by the fringes of Carlton – the Italian precinct, established by immigrants as part of the government's White Australia policy following World War II – and through the CBD, a stone's throw from Chinatown, where Chinese immigrants first settled in the 1850s during the gold rush.[2]

Continuing on, I would cross through West Melbourne, resisting the temptation to take a leisurely detour to the fashionable bayside suburbs of St Kilda and Elwood, inhabited by Jewish refugees and Holocaust survivors in the 1950s.

Exiting the city precinct, I would hit the truck path to Footscray Rd, cross the Maribyrnong River (waving to the Lonely Planet head office to the left as I did so, itself founded by two immigrants from the UK, Tony and Maureen Wheeler) before arriving in Footscray, where the main streets bustle with Vietnamese restaurants (a legacy of Vietnamese migration following the war in the 1970s), and recently established African cafés. Finally, I would reach Maidstone, where I would find the rather misnamed immigration centre, surrounded by razor wire and 'home' to people from places such as Afghanistan, Iran and Iraq.

Having mapped my course, there was only one more thing to do – find the name of someone at the detention centre I could visit. I emailed a contact who could hopefully help, and the next morning I received a reply:

> At the moment, supporters of people in the Maribyrnong camp are in the unusual position of having many offers of help from visitors while at the same time the refugee (as opposed to the overstayer[3] and common criminal) population of the centre has shrunk to fewer than 10 people.
>
> This is because some people have been released while others have been packed off to the much less accessible Baxter centre in Port Augusta.[4] Many also remain on the Pacific island of Nauru.[5] Of course

---

2. By 1861 there were 38,348 Chinese immigrants in Australia – 38,337 men but only 11 women.
3. 'Overstayers' are those who overstay their visa. Frequent overstayers in Australia include British and New Zealand backpackers, yet strangely, according to a lobby-group source, no 'Anglo' person has ever been detained for overstaying their visa, with the exception of a North American tourist who arrived drunk at the airport and tried to punch a passport control officer. He was detained overnight, but left for home the following day.

it's much less practical to try to visit people there (the cynical might suggest that's one reason for shifting these poor unfortunates out of town!). Certainly many of the detainees there feel as if they are invisible – non-persons, no-one even knows they are there. Can I suggest that you get the name of someone in one of those centres, write to them and make friends that way? It means just so much to these poor people – and can literally be a lifeline.

Some days later I had a name and an address. Initially, all I'd wanted to do was draw a virtual rubber stamp with my car (a pretty harmless ambition) – and here I was, settling down to write a letter to a new pen friend in the middle of the desert...

But even though my attempts at travelling physically were being thwarted, an opportunity had appeared that somehow captured, for me, the spirit of Experimental Travel: being open to others, and allowing yourself to explore – and celebrate – the unexpected.

Having sealed and stamped the envelope, I walked to the nearest letter box and sent it off. And then I went home. Because I could.

THE JOURNEY OF ALADDIN & HIS CAT

If Aladdin Sisalem had been lucky enough to have a magic carpet, his life would have been all the easier. Alas, the 20-something Palestinian-born man spent four years in search of a country that could offer him a home. As the sole resident on the remote Manus Island detention camp, Aladdin spent 18 months of effective solitary confinement while waiting for his claim to be processed. During this time he befriended a stray cat he called Honey. Following a media uproar when his lonely plight was discovered, Aladdin was finally approved entry to Australia. However, strict quarantine laws prevented Honey accompanying him. In a strange show of solidarity, a group that comprised both left-wing political groups and a right-wing talkback radio host lobbied to raise money so that the cat could spend the requisite time in quarantine and thus join Aladdin in Australia. Some months later, Honey was also freed.

---

4. Port Augusta (population 14,000) is in South Australia, 300km north of Adelaide, and is a pass-through point for travellers crossing the Nullabor Plain to Western Australia, or going to Alice Springs in the Northern Territory. According to one refugee lobby group, the centre is protected by a 10,000-volt electric fence, said to be stronger than the fences that surround Australia's high-security prisons. **5.** In November 2003, the Australia government retrospectively excised almost 4000 islands from Australia's northern migration zone to stop a boatload of around 20 suspected asylum seekers from applying for refugee status (as reported in www.theage.com.au). In an attempt to keep asylum seekers out of Australian territory, they also 'outsourced' immigration detention facilities to the tiny Pacific island of Manus (in the cash-strapped nation of Papua New Guinea), and on Nauru, a barren island nation that made – and squandered – a fortune from mining bird droppings for phosphate.

HYPOTHESIS: Have a budget day-spa experience at the house of a friend.

APPARATUS: A friend who has a bathroom or, better yet, a spa. (Scandinavian types would be well advised to seek out a sauna.)

METHOD: Citing an invented burst water pipe or lack of hot water, invite yourself to take a bath at the house of one of your friends. Take along all the equipment you would use in a spa: soap, shampoo, towel, bathrobe, relaxing music, candles, seaweed scrub, champagne etc. Consider receiving guests. Feel free to sing.

INTRODUCTORY NOTES:

This game was first developed during a period of economic crisis in 1992 and published in a special issue of *Cahiers du Latourex* devoted to crisis tourism. Chic day spas offer a luxurious and fashionable solution to the stress of urban living, but they come with a hefty price tag. Thalasso Experimental is a mischievous way to enjoy a day-spa experience on a small budget, while also allowing you to subvert etiquette and invade the most private room of the house.

Thalasso travel gets the traveller out of their safety zone (and out of their clothes!). This experiment could well inspire a revival of the communal bathhouses common to Japan, the Middle East and some Native American traditions. But whether one bathes alone, or with friends, the therapeutic effects of warm water in a tranquil setting should not be underestimated. For optimum comfort try to avoid the 'tap end'.

LABORATORY RESULTS

Courtesy of Experimental Tourist Michael Clerizo, London, UK.

I am standing in the middle of a Chinese restaurant, pleading with the owner to let me use his shower. The owner, William, from Hong Kong, is one of my closest friends. Last year, I was the first person he told when he became engaged to his girlfriend, Mandy, from Beijing.

Fibbing madly, I say, 'We've got the builders in and they're painting the ceiling in the bathroom. I can't take a shower or shave and I have a meeting in the West End. Can I use yours?'

Even though it's 11am and William is preparing for lunch, he kindly agrees. We leap into his people-mover and drive round to his house.

On the way I ask if his shower has any idiosyncrasies. Does the hot-water tap require a gentle nudge before it will turn on? Does the shower curtain go inside or outside the tub? How many minutes does the hot water last? I take long showers. Also, I don't trust my footing on unfamiliar, wet surfaces. Does he have a shower mat? Other people's bathrooms are quirky and sometimes treacherous places, and I like to be prepared.

William is reassuring. Everything in his bathroom functions smoothly. The hot water will last for at least half an hour. There is a screen, not a curtain, and yes, he does have a shower mat.

Arriving at William's I discover that the bathroom is a bright-yellow and blue room. Eleven orange ceramic frogs are arranged around one corner of the bathtub. Eleven white candles are arranged around the diagonally opposite corner, at the head of the tub.

A shelf over the toilet is full of bottles and jars. Some I recognise but others are unfamiliar. The latter have something in common with William and Mandy – they're all from China.

I'm curious to know what's inside these exotic vessels but all the labels are in Chinese. For a moment I hesitate. Then I open each one, peer inside and inhale, hoping to recognise a scent. There are nine in total, and I can identify the contents of only two: one jar has a pale-green creamy liquid with a jasmine aroma; the other is a small blue bottle containing bath salts.

I opt for a bath instead of a shower and turn on the taps. After tipping in the bath salts I add a few drops of the jasmine cream. Hey, why not? I've always loved jasmine tea.

As the tub fills with water, the room fills with the fragrance of jasmine. I decide to go for the full effect. Using some matches I find in the cabinet over the sink, I light the candles on the corner of the tub.

Luxuriating in the hot, scented water, I shave, something I always do in the bath or shower, and then lie back and relax. I glance up at the still unknown bottles on the shelf and consider learning Chinese…

'Other people's bathrooms are quirky and sometimes
treacherous places, and I like to be prepared.'

WATER CURE

*The French writer Valéry Larbaud was the son of the manager of Vichy, the famous
spring where the moneyed classes went to 'take the waters'. One summer in Paris,
Larbaud and his friends, who were mostly artists and writers, organised a 'water cure'
of several days along the Champs-Élysées, drinking 'a quart of Vichy' every hour in a
different café. Larbaud later described the game in his novel Jaune, Bleu, Blanc.*

travel pursuit

HYPOTHESIS: Follow in someone else's footsteps.

APPARATUS: A trench coat, a camera and a newspaper with holes cut out for your eyes.

METHOD: Follow some friends when they go on holiday and don't let them out of your sight. Take photographs of them using a telephoto lens. On their return home, consider welcoming them with a slideshow of their holiday. Joël Henry suggests that unless you are a professional detective, you may find it easier to simply pick someone at random from a crowd and follow them to see where you end up.

Note: this experiment can also be applied to day trips and short outings.

INTRODUCTORY NOTES:

Clearly it's important to make a distinction between following someone in a playful way and outright stalking. Stakeouts, phone taps and shopping for infrared glasses are all signs that things have gone too far.

For inspiration you might try studying the works of the French artist Sophie Calle. When Calle returned to Paris after a seven-year absence, she rediscovered the city by following people at random. These expeditions led to the publication of *Suite Venitienne* in 1979, in which Calle follows an attractive-looking man to Venice. Once there, she tracks down where he is staying and follows him from a distance, taking notes and photographs and speaking to everyone he interacts with, until an accidental meeting leads her to abandon the chase. Later, in 1981, she hired a detective to follow and photograph her for a week.[1] As one might imagine, Calle's artistic adventures occasionally resulted in legal difficulties.[2]

1. The name of the work is, aptly enough, *The Detective*. **2.** In 1983 Calle found an address book, photocopied it and returned it to the owner. She then contacted the people listed in the book, and built up a portrait of the address book's owner through the impressions of his friends and colleagues. Her findings were published in *La Libération* newspaper. The owner of the address book, a documentary filmmaker called Pierre Baudry, didn't enjoy being the subject of Calle's artistic inquiry, and threatened to sue her for invasion of privacy.

I must admit I find the idea of tailing a total stranger in the street a trifle distasteful. There's a very real risk of frightening your target, and even when one's motivation is purely scientific it is still an invasion of their privacy. Thus I begin my experiment by considering the type of individual I will have the least scruples in following. The conclusion is elementary: it should be someone already well versed in the covert arts of surveillance – a private detective. In a thrilling version of the hunter becoming the hunted, a man follows a man who is following him – an inversion of the artist Sophie Calle's idea of having herself followed by a detective and turning the detective's report into her autobiography. On that occasion it was the Duluc detective agency in Paris that took the case – quite a recommendation – so that's where I begin my own private investigation. There's no question of a smokescreen, come what may; no false moustache or sunglasses for me. Instead, I will bring along my folding bicycle for added mobility or to make a quick getaway if things get dicey.

The following morning, at 0846 hours, I take up my vantage point in a café on Rue du Louvre, staking out the apartment building at Number 18. I have a good angle on the garage door, which has a blue neon sign on it: 'Duluc Detectives', it reads. What the blazes is a real detective supposed to look like? The idea I've formed in my mind is a hodgepodge of all the crime shows and books I've seen and read: a lone wolf with the looks of a leading man, badly shaven and dressed in a crumpled trench coat. But in real life it will most likely be someone able to blend into a crowd, a chameleon. I'll have to look sharp if I am going to sniff him out among those leaving the apartment building.

0928 hours: Three teens with backpacks. Too young.

1037 hours: An elegant woman carrying shopping bags from La Samaritaine. Not really how I imagined my sleuth (unless it's a cover).

1044 hours: A man in a blue apron. He lights a cigarette, smokes it and re-enters the building.

1102 hours: A man aged 30 to 40, wearing a jacket and tie, with a confident stride. Perhaps a lawyer or professor of mathematics. He'll do as my private dick. He crosses the street and heads my way. I pay for my coffee and hightail it out of there, but my detective is already kickstarting a scooter parked on the sidewalk in front of where I'd been seated. Even if I pedal my bike furiously, he'll have already shaken me.

I spend two hours scrutinising the same minute cross-section of Paris like a hawk: a doorway and several yards of sidewalk. Although this fierce concentration allows me to observe several micro-events I may not have otherwise noticed, it is high time for a change of scenery.

There's no shortage of detective agencies in Paris – according to the Yellow Pages, there are more than 100. Most of them, however, are fly-by-night. I cycle for miles across Paris, only to find myself, more often than not, face to face with an anonymous doorway, most notably in the case of the agency called Detectives for Any Occasion, on Rue Lecourbe. I am happy enough to be able to photograph the sign, but the agency itself is at the far end of a courtyard and I need to know the code to enter the glass door.

I'm unable to tail anyone for very long. You can't just improvise being a private detective – it's a profession. But I enjoy a delightful bicycle ride through Paris, going from one agency's address to the next, stopping here and there for a stakeout. I learn how difficult it is to loiter in the street without drawing the curious attention of passers-by, or, more to the point, without seeming suspicious. I have to resort to my sense of cunning.

I huddle on the marble stairway of Nôtre-Dame-des-Champs, keeping an eye on the glassed entranceway of ABAC Detectives on the opposite side of Boulevard de Montparnasse. Seated on a bench on the Champs-Élysées, I stake out the Cabinet Martin agency by peeking over the top of my newspaper. I spend some time sketching the splendid porch of Building 18 on Place Vendôme, which houses not only the Nobel & Trevits agency but also, on the ground floor, the deluxe boutiques of the Italian jeweler Bulgari and the Swiss watchmaker Patek Philippe. At the Goutte d'Or it is a different story. In order to keep an eye on the comings and goings at Bensaïd Investigations on Rue de Suez, I have to roll up my sleeves and get my hands dirty by pretending to repair my bicycle on the sidewalk, surrounded by the aromas of spices from faraway and the endless flow of robed men calling to each other in all the languages of Africa.

My Travel Pursuit results in the invention of a new game: discovering a city according to the particular geography of its detective agencies.

FIND THAT DETECTIVE!

Those considering Travel Pursuit might like to bone up on the detective genre beforehand. The following literary characters are highly recommended for their skills of detection:

Arthur Conan Doyle: the genre was pioneered by **Sherlock Holmes** and his long-time colleague **Doctor Watson**. Holmesian societies around the world continue to orchestrate themed trips and gatherings.

Agatha Christie: Hercule Poirot and the not-so-dainty **Miss Marple**, supposedly based on Christie's own grandmother, excel at solving sordid middle-class, suburban crimes.

Arthur W Upfield: an Aboriginal detective of mixed origins, **Bony** (aka Detective Inspector Napoleon Bonaparte) investigated 29 baffling cases, mostly in outback Australia.

Alexander McCall Smith: the traditionally built **Mma Ramotswe** of the No. 1 Ladies Detective Agency solves crime and serves bush tea while ruminating on issues of morality in Botswana.

TRIP POKER

HYPOTHESIS: Take a gamble on a trip.

APPARATUS: Four people, one dice, a poker face.

METHOD: Trip Poker is a travel game for four or more people. Your itinerary in this instance is created by rolling a dice, but you can easily adapt the rules to a game of poker.

1) The person who rolls the highest number wins the first round and gets to choose the destination. The destination should lie within a specified distance of where the game is being played, eg 500km.

2) The winner of the second roll decides the date of the weekend away.

3) The winner of the third roll determines the type of accommodation, eg hotel, camping, in the car, at someone's house, under the stars, no accommodation – and no sleep!

4) The person who loses the last roll of the dice pays for the weekend.

INTRODUCTORY NOTES:

Unlike your average poker game, this one uses dice, not cards. While the rules can be altered if playing with cards, for simplicity's sake we'd recommend avoiding a deck created by pranksters of the art movement Fluxus – they tend to have 52 jokers…

Playing Trip Poker is a real *wild card* – there's no knowing where you'll end up, and, if the *chips are down*, there's no *passing the buck*. Unlike normal poker, there's no clear winner in this game; you're all in it together, which certainly helps to *up the ante*. That said, there is a clear loser, as those travel expenses sure do *stack up*. If you're really broke, consider asking your fellow card-sharks to lend you a *hand*.

LABORATORY RESULTS
Courtesy of Experimental Tourist Jöel Henry,
Strasbourg, France.

There were four of us around the table: our friends Robert and Christine and Maïa and myself. There was green baize, subdued lighting and a bottle of very old whisky. Trip poker is no laughing matter – the rounds may be very short but it's a dangerous game that can take you far and cost you dearly.

Thanks to the modest roll of a four, I won the first round and with it the stake: the chance to choose the destination for our weekend break together. After a quick glance at an atlas to check out the 500km limit, I chose Geneva, a city none of us had visited before.

Maïa won the second round with a straight six, and the responsibility fell to her to choose the date for the weekend. She cannot bear loud parties, particularly those on New Year's Eve, which we have celebrated for years with old college friends to an unchanging formula: the consumption of highly calorific and expensive food, depressing discussions about the passing of time and Abba on repeat, all washed down with gallons of champagne. Teetotaller Maïa attends these annual drinking sessions under sufferance. So the traitor took advantage of the situation and chose New Year's Eve for our little trip, despite the protestations of the three other contestants. In our defence we cited Geneva's insipid partying reputation and the city's polar temperatures at the end of December, but the rules of the game were on Maïa's side and she wouldn't budge.

Christine won the third roll of the dice and therefore got to choose the type of accommodation. She decided without hesitation that we would sleep in the car. This was tactical rather than stingy: she's in charge of household finances, and she knew that there was a 50 per cent chance that she and Robert would have to foot the bill. And hotels in Geneva don't come cheap...

'But we'll freeze to death,' complained Robert.'We'll take thermal blankets,' she replied firmly.

> 'Despite its innocent exterior, Trip Poker is a cousin of Russian roulette.'

It must be said that, though a charming man, Robert is somewhat of a spendthrift and his latest folly, the purchase of a new Mini Cooper with all the extras ('a childhood dream'), had cleaned them out for a few years. So the last round was played in an atmosphere of extreme tension, until I rolled the dice with a faulty hand and my pitiful one put an end to the suspense.

So to sum up, unless Switzerland becomes a totalitarian state cut off from the rest of the world, the four of us will celebrate next New Year's Eve in Geneva, sleeping in minus 15°C temperatures in a Mini Cooper – our only option, as Maïa and I, as ecological fundamentalists, have long forsaken car ownership. And I shall be footing the bill. Make no mistake, despite its innocent exterior, Trip Poker is a cousin of Russian roulette.

12

TRAVEL

HYPOTHESIS: Use the number 12 to compose a travel itinerary.

APPARATUS: A map, timetable or travel plan that relates to the number 12.

METHOD: Twelve is a tremendously flexible number, able to accommodate a variety of Experimental Travel forms. Examples include the following:

- Take a train that leaves at 12.12 and get off at the 12th stop.
- Walk or swim along the 12th line of latitude.
- Undertake a tour of hotels, only staying in room number 12.
- Begin a round-the-world trip with only 12 units of currency in your pocket (eg £12, $12 or €12).
- Journey along motorway or highway number 12.

INTRODUCTORY NOTES:

Twelve Travel[1] was inspired by 'dodecaphony' or serial music, the 12-tone method of musical composition developed by the controversial Austrian composer Arnold Schönberg (1874–1951). When Schönberg abandoned tonality in favour of his mathematical technique (which might be described as 'composition with constraints'), he did to music what the Cubist painters did to perspective – and was received with similar levels of popularity. Schönberg was one of the most influential composers of modern times, but his work was rarely performed in his lifetime and was continuously attacked by critics, many of whom had never even heard it. Interestingly enough, Schönberg is said to have suffered from fear of the number 13 (triskaidekaphobia).

1 Also known as *Dodecatourisme* or Serial Travel.

Twelve can be a difficult number, at least when it comes to British train timetables. I know, because I phoned National Rail enquiries and asked the 'client services representative' to find me 'A train that left a station at 12 minutes after any hour'.

Helpful, if somewhat perplexed, the cheery young man explained, 'Our computers aren't set up to find trains that leave at specific times unless you tell us the station you're travelling from.'

'Okay, I said, 'find me a train leaving Euston Station at 12 minutes after any hour.'

'Going where, sir?'

'Anywhere that's 12 stops from Euston.'

'You'll have to be more specific, sir.'

He still sounded sincere but I sensed a hint of dread in his voice. He probably thought, 'This a real nutcase. How many hours will I be stuck on the phone with him?' I apologised for wasting his time and said goodbye.

Next, I tried the local library. The reference room has a book of up-to-date train timetables, but after an hour of hunting through hundreds of pages of small print, *Finnegans Wake* seemed like an easy vacation read. I gave up again.

Then, as I was walking through my local London Underground station, I found the answer. Like a sign from a greater power, a poster appeared before me, declaring that, 'Trains depart every 12 minutes' from Mill Hill East, a stop on the Northern Line.

All I had to do was jump on a train at Mill Hill East and travel for 12 stops.

Twelve stops after Mill Hill East was Moorgate, and disappointment, for it is in London's financial district. Stockbrokers and money managers are fine by me but the streetscape is boring. It has exactly the same coffee bars and shops you see in any other part of the city centre. Every façade has been designed by consultancies that follow orthodoxy masquerading as creativity.

I decided to improvise, and headed back to the Northern Line. Twelve stops south of Moorgate is the quaintly named Tooting Bec. The station's interior is covered in white, black, grey, green and indigo tiles, while in contrast the exterior is a brutal two-storey concrete wedge – but the surrounding streetscape is fabulous!

I feel quietly confident in saying that there has never been a design consultant anywhere near Tooting Bec. The suburb is full of small businesses that

unselfconsciously mark out their territory. The atmosphere is relaxed and friendly.

In the Newsflash Newsagent the owner and I chatted about pop star Michael Jackson's latest legal predicament.

Nearby, Benett's International store had a sign optimistically proclaiming itself 'The place to be. English, Asian, Sri Lankan Groceries, News, Off-licence, CD Video and Audio (Tamil)'.

The Café Espresso boasted that it served 'Hot and cold meals cooked to the highest standards'.

At the local Asian centre a sign announced that the vegetarian lunch club meets every day; the nonvegetarian club meets only on Saturdays.

Holy Trinity, the parish church, had published a one-page history which stated that 'There is little in the way of outstanding historical events in the history of this parish'.

Walking back to the station, I passed the House Clearance Centre, which 'Wanted All Household Furniture and Electrical'. On the pavement was an upright piano. I played a few bars of 'Good Golly Miss Molly'. It wasn't quite up to Schönberg's standard, but no-one minded.

VOYAGE TO THE

HYPOTHESIS: Explore what lies at the end of the line.

APPARATUS: A form of transport, eg train, ferry, car.

METHOD: Take a suburban train out of the city and travel to the end of the line. If no train is available, choose another form of transport. If possible, find accommodation to stay the night and explore the area that you find yourself in.

END OF THE LINE

INTRODUCTORY NOTES:

Taking a Voyage to the End of the Line is the perfect way to re-create a sense of adventure in your own town. You get to travel to places you would otherwise never go to, but depending on your mode of transport, it can take you a lot further than you might think...

In 1492 Christopher Columbus, one of the most famous Experimental Travellers of all time, took a boat to the end of the line. At the time, much of the Western world had accepted a rather eccentric theory that the world was spherical,[1] but some sceptics (and the Catholic Church) were clinging to the established truth: the world was flat and Christopher Columbus was going to sail right off the end of it (thus proving rather definitively that 'pride comes before a fall'). Columbus got lucky – the world was round – but he missed his intended destination (Asia) by a continent or two, winding up instead in the Americas.[2] The native inhabitants were not so lucky, as the arrival of Columbus and his pals resulted in the destruction of life as they had known it. The lesson to be learnt? A Voyage to the End of the Line, while inspiring and romantic, can have dangerous and unintended consequences. Try to travel lightly and leave only footprints behind.

1. In fact the debate had been going on for some time, as the first known theorist to suggest the earth was round was Aristotle. **2.** An incident that might be described as 'serendipitous travel' (see Chance Travel on p90).

LABORATORY RESULTS

Courtesy of Experimental Tourist Rachael Antony, Stony Point, Australia.

Great journeys always seem to entail early rising, so in keeping with the tradition of the explorers who went before us we dutifully set our alarm clocks; this was to be our only conventional act in an otherwise nonsensical expedition. Of course, being underemployed arty types, we were unaccustomed to what others knew as the 'morning', and thus it was with sleepy eyes and fuzzy heads that Janet, Dave and I approached Flinders Street train station at 7.30am the next day. Our goal was to travel to the end of the line – the intriguingly named Stony Point – and make a film, the details and motivations of which were unclear.

We took the regular train as far as it would go, then changed to another, less-frequent diesel version and chug-chugged our way to the end of the line... Having arrived, we stopped at the sole sign of civilisation, a small general store, where we ordered a hot cup of tea, debated the relative 'stoniness' of Stony Point ('I've seen stonier,' said Dave, thoughtfully) and waited for the morning fog to clear from the sea.

Thus revived, we set off carrying the necessities of the day: Dave had brought along his old 16mm hand-held camera; Janet, somewhat impractically, was dragging a large blue beanbag; while I had packed a *Famous Five*-style picnic lunch, an oversized pair of green novelty sunglasses, a blue water pistol and a coconut bra (just in case). Our wanderings took us to a bleak and lonely seascape where we improvised an Ingmar Bergman-inspired exchange between Dave and Janet, punctuated with intense looks and 'stony' silences, followed by a slightly strange and rather incomprehensible love story between Janet and the beanbag. Heading off once more, we came across a spooky, seemingly desolate military base before finding a scenic nature reserve where we rested – Dave and I on the damp emerald grass, Janet on her beanbag – in a dappled sunny hollow and watched the butterflies...

Some hours later, drowsy from the afternoon sun, Janet dozed on the train trip back to the urban jungle, while Dave and I mused on the End of the Line and the world we had found there. 'But David,' I said, 'where was the point?' He looked deep into my eyes, stroking an imaginary beard that lent him an air of wisdom beyond his age, 'Rachael,' he replied, 'there is no point. It just is.'

'I had packed a *Famous Five*-style picnic lunch,
an oversized pair of green novelty sunglasses, a blue
water pistol and a coconut bra (just in case).'

APPENDICES

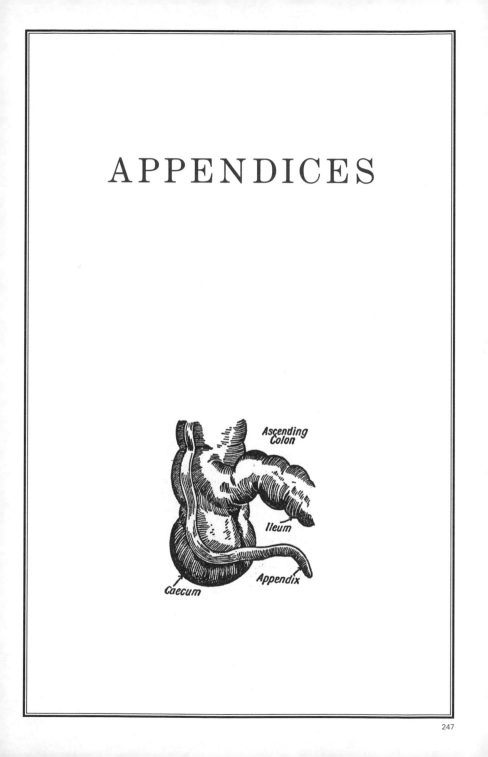

LONELY PLANET
and
YELLOW ARROW
invite you to participate in a
Global Public Art Project

find out more at
www.lonelyplanet.com/experimentaltravel

YELLOW ARROW

TRAVEL IS AN ARTISTIC ACT

While a traditional guidebook can get you around the highlights and top attractions, you'll often find yourself jostling for space with hordes of other tourists all seeking the same experience. Yellow Arrow[1] allows you to access a more personal, unique and random experience of place. With a growing international community of arrow authors, Yellow Arrow is the first global public art project and is collaboratively creating a M.A.A.P.[2] of the world's most personally significant spaces.

Here is how it works: Find a place that speaks to you, something you want to point out, a detail in your environment that counts. Mark that place with the Yellow Arrow.[3] Once you have placed your arrow, send an SMS to the Yellow Arrow number (see the back of the sticker for detailed information). Start with the arrow's unique code, followed by a message about the place you've chosen. Your text will be saved on the spot. Keep your eyes open for others' Yellow Arrows. When you encounter one, SMS its code to the Yellow Arrow number and the message of the arrow will be sent immediately to your phone. You can also share your arrows online. Log onto My Arrows at www.yellowarrow.net to contribute photos and maps to the global gallery.

GETTING THE POINT

What makes an attraction? When does an object become art? Who says what counts? Duchamp famously dragged a bottle rack—now *The Bottle Rack*—into a gallery. Only his signature separated the contraption from duplicates that anyone could buy in a department store. You might say it was his intention alone that transformed the object into art. Or you might say that it was a load of nonsense. For the romantic, Yellow Arrow claims an analogous power to mystically change the mundane into the artistic, but beyond the gallery and with a somewhat more technical means of autograph. For the less serious, Yellow Arrow is a whimsical way to memorialise a thought about a specific location.

In a word, the Yellow Arrow simply says 'this'. This thing. This way. Historically speaking, the arrow has been widely considered the most fundamental symbol of human communication, though there is some debate as to when and where the icon first emerged. Imagine a stooped, hairy man in the caves at Lascaux using a charred stick to first point out, then trace a bulge on the wall that looked to him like a bison. Grunting, 'This. Check this out.'

Zoom forward to the 1970s, when NASA, confident that extraterrestrials would understand the arrow, launched it deep into space. The Pioneer 10, which now floats on its own experimental tourist voyage, unmanned and drifting beyond the orbit of Pluto, was a sort of 'message in a bottle' aimed at aliens. Prominent among other artefacts, the vessel was equipped with a plaque that included the image of two nudes flanking a map of our solar system. A parabolic arrow stretched from an illustration of the Pioneer 10 back to Earth. The idea was that even a Martian would get the point.

Yellow Arrow builds on the history of this apparently universal symbol while simultaneously empowering local people to tell local stories. United around pointing out what counts, a new sub-culture has formed that crosses national borders. Whether capturing ephemeral experience (the bottle rack) or making collective memories of place accessible (the message in a bottle) the Yellow Arrow is a tool for uncovering the secret life of cities around the world.

1. Yellow Arrow™ is a registered trademark of Counts Media, Inc. www.yellowarrow.net.

2. 'Massively Authored Artistic Project' (a term coined by the inventors of Yellow Arrow).

3. Note: please do not vandalise public or private property. Ask permission first!

IMAGES FROM THE GLOBAL GALLERY

Courtesy of Yellow Arrow authors around the world.

#g0476 by panda. *Spring & Mulberry Sts, New York, NY, USA.* Sage advice: never grow up too much.

#m5096 by jshapes. *Emilio Carranza y Iturbide in Puerto Vallarta, Mexico.* To me, this boot is more beautiful than any famous painting, or any work in a museum.

#a8760 by livia. *Edgeware Rd, London, UK.* Ranoush is 2 mins down the road, best Lebanese takeaway in London.

#g7a92 by stan. *Wijk aan Zee in Haarlem, Netherlands.* Feel the wind. Hear the energy.

#g0682 by triplll. *The beach, Aruba, Caribbean.* Abundant messages from past visitors. Clearly, Andy Goldsworthy was here.

#p1d73 by cdp. *Friedbergstraße, Berlin, Germany.* Meine nachbarin steht auf. My neighbor wakes up.

#d5196 by daveking. *Near Degraves St, Melbourne, Australia.* Swivel and pivot to see graf-expressionism. Come back soon – this laneway breathes urban art.

#p6035 by ph.urban. *Totentanz, Basel, Switzerland.* Basel ist ein Zoo – überall kleine Stangenzebras. Basel is a Zoo — everywhere there are little zebra poles.

#m81w8 by daveking. *Bourke & Swanston Sts, Melbourne, Australia.* The skeletal guardians of city shopping. Peering and poking

#w2tm8 by skolgen. *Academy of Fine Arts, Antwerp, Belgium.* A piece of art blocks the Academy of Fine Arts.

#mgwp0 by urbanite. *Sydhavnsgade, Copenhagen, Denmark.* One yellow arrow found another. A safe place for the first YA in Copenhagen, next to the home of urbanites.org.

#gd4a3 by Vid. *Orrs Mills & Old Pleasant Hill Rds, Mountainville, NY, USA.* The river permeates all. Stand here long enough and it will surely consume you, too. Take a pebble to remember.

#mptp4 by sdoolin. *Dead Sea, Jordan.* The lowest and saltiest place on earth: Dead Sea, Jordan.

#gjwa3 by cook. *12th & Euclid, Cleveland, OH, USA.* 'We must never forget that art is not a form of propaganda; it is a form of truth.' – John F Kennedy, 26 October, 1963.

THE PUZZLE ARROW
Courtesy of Yellow Arrow author 'Insley', Boston, USA.

'Your City/My City' is a puzzle spread across Boston using Yellow Arrows. The message on each arrow consists of a short statement, followed by a series of numbers and the clue leading to the next arrow. Each number corresponds to one of the words on the arrow. For example, the statement on arrow #tmtp5 is 'You see. You show.' and the numbers are 14, 19, 10, 11. Thus, You = 14, See = 19, You = 10, Show = 11. When all the arrows have been found, the user can piece together a short paragraph about the city by organising the words according to their numbers, 1-34 (see the legend below).

START:

#wa515 Harvard Square T station
The story for this place is part of a bigger story. Follow the arrows. Use the numbers to put the words in order. I'll meet you at the end. Next arrow: Harvard Sq. Au Bon Pain. Underneath middle chessboard.

#tmtp5 at Harvard Square
You see. You show. 14, 19, 10, 11. Next arrow: Central Sq. 630 Mass Ave. Payphone.

#d5010 at Central Square
If I ride, will you look? 23, 24, 34, 30, 26, 32. Next arrow: MIT. 84 Mass Ave. Trash can at entrance.

#j90p9 at MIT
Work is us. 5, 2, 8. 407. Newbury. Other Side. Door."

#p6214 at Newbury
An art made of Boston. 3, 4, 6, 7, 1. Next arrow: 755 Boylston. Mailbox.

#j2m24 at 755 Boylston
I'll show you what I...if you... 16, 25, 26, 27, 28, 9, 10. Next arrow: 15 Arlington. Ritz Hotel. Lampost base.

#pjg95 at Ritz Hotel
What to see? The real city. 13, 18, 29, 20, 21, 22. 427. Mass Ave. Wallys Cafe. Entrance sign.

#dmg92 at Wally's Café
You. Me. Let's see. 31, 12, 33, 15. Next arrow: 33 Stanhope St. 33 Restaurant. Fire hydrant.

#pm162 at 33 Restaurant
Start! 17.

THE LEGEND:

1. Boston
2. is
3. an
4. art
5. work
6. made
7. of
8. us.
9. If
10. you
11. show
12. me
13. what
14. you
15. see,
16. I'll
17. start
18. to
19. see
20. the
21. real
22. city.
23. If
24. I
25. show
26. you
27. what
28. I
29. see,
30. will
31. you
32. look?
33. Let's
34. ride.

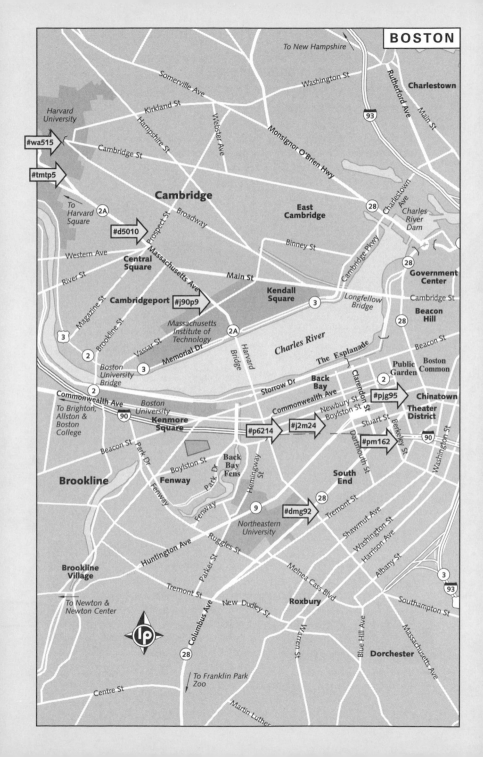

✦❀✦

THE LINKED ARROW
Courtesy of Yellow Arrow, New York, USA.

❀❀❀

With the six stickers in this book, author your own experimental adventure. Create a guided experience for someone through a special place by linking Yellow Arrows together. For inspriation, check out this tour through Queens, NY, USA.

#a0185. You have arrived at one of NYC's great cultural spaces. But there is another lesser-known centre of creative activity behind you. Turn around, walk across street to the large mural. The next Yellow Arrow has 5Pointz.

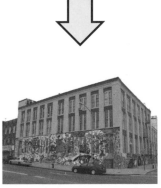

You turn around and see the mural across the street.

#t0jg1. You are on your way to the Phun Factory, one of NYC's few sanctioned centres for graffiti. Walk to the corner and turn right. The next Yellow Arrow is on the base of the third support for the elevated train.

#pt419. Keep moving forward. Turn right into parking lot entrance. The Yellow Arrow that will lead you on your ascent is on a pole under the sign 'painting with permits only'.

Down the street to the right from the corner, you notice the support bases for the elevated train.

You look towards the corner and see the elevated train.

You enter the wildly colourful parking lot of the Phun Factory and approach the sign in front of you.

#m1247. You have permission to climb the stairs. Don't worry, it's cool with the Phun Factory. Notice the gallery of work as you ascend. The Yellow Arrow is near the Yellow Face.

#mp213. One foot after the other, climb safely. One hand after the other on the ladder at the end until you get to the roof. Approach Manhattan for the final message.

#gd463. You see your starting point from a new perspective. Queens and Manhattan melt into one magnificent range of mountains to be scaled. There is a Yellow Arrow atop the Chrysler building. Squint and you can see it.

YELLOW ARROW & MODERN PSYCHOGEOGRAPHY

Current approaches to Psychogeography (see p23) vary, and include artistic, political, philosophical and scientific work in fields ranging from architecture to street art. Yellow Arrow first emerged at the Glowlab psy.geo Conflux, an annual gathering of Psychogeographers from around the world, in New York City in May, 2004. For more info: www.glowlab.com.

THE TRAVEL PIE:

10,000,000,000
IMPOSSIBLE JOURNEYS

In 1961 the French Oulipo writer Raymond Queneau (the author of *Zazie dans le métro*) published *One Hundred Million Million Poems (Cent Mille Milliards de Poèmes)*, a set of 10 sonnets, each presented on a separate page. Inspired by children's books, each page is split into 14 strips, with a separate strip for each line, the idea being that you can flip the strips and combine the lines, thus creating your own sonnets. The book's title comes from the number of potential poems the book contains – 100,000,000,000,000 (10^{14}). Queneau estimated that it would take approximately 200 million years to read all the possible combinations. Our Travel Pie is based on the same principle but has only 10 lines per page – we still think there are enough slices to keep you busy for the next couple of hundred million years anyway.

DIRECTIONS FOR USE

1) Take a pair of scissors.
2) Slice the 'pie' by cutting the pages along the dotted lines.
3) Flip the strips according to your wishes and create your own delicious travel treat.

TRAVEL TYPE:	SUMMER HOLIDAY
TRAVEL TO:	MONGOLIA
BY:	DONKEY
WEARING:	A WHITE LINEN SUIT
CARRYING:	A BRIEFCASE
STAYING IN:	A YURT
DINING ON:	DRIED YAK
FOR:	TWO WEEKS
WITH:	TRAVELLING NOMADS
WHILE THERE:	BEGIN WRITING YOUR MEMOIRS

TRAVEL TYPE: **FIND YOURSELF**

 -

TRAVEL TO: **BERLIN**

BY: **STEAM TRAIN**

WEARING: **GOTHIC-PUNK**

CARRYING: **A BACKPACK**

STAYING IN: **A SQUAT**

DINING ON: **FELAFEL**

FOR: **SIX MONTHS**

WITH: **NOBODY**

WHILE THERE: **JOIN AN ANARCHIC ARTS COLLECTIVE**

| TRAVEL TYPE: | SCIENTIFIC EXPEDITION |

✂

| TRAVEL TO: | SOMEWHERE IN AFRICA |

| BY: | HOT-AIR BALLOON |

| WEARING: | SAFARI GEAR |

| CARRYING: | LARGE AND AWKWARD AMOUNTS OF POINTLESS EQUIPMENT |

| STAYING IN: | A 4WD |

| DINING ON: | BEEF JERKY |

| FOR: | FOUR WEEKS |

| WITH: | COLLEAGUES |

| WHILE THERE: | MAKE A REMARKABLE DISCOVERY |

TRAVEL TYPE: ROMANTIC GETAWAY

✂ -

TRAVEL TO: ICELAND

- -

BY: MERCEDES-BENZ

- -

WEARING: FURS

- -

CARRYING: A VIOLA

- -

STAYING IN: A GRAND HOTEL

- -

DINING ON: ROOM SERVICE

- -

FOR: A WEEKEND

- -

WITH: A MYSTERIOUS STRANGER

- -

WHILE THERE: PHOTOGRAPH FEET

TRAVEL TYPE: EMIGRATE

✂

TRAVEL TO: A SOUTH AMERICAN CAPITAL CITY

BY: TAXI THROUGH THE ANDES

WEARING: DARK GLASSES

CARRYING: AN OLD PHOTO ALBUM

STAYING IN: AN ABANDONED 18TH-CENTURY APARTMENT

DINING ON: OVERSIZED STEAK

FOR: EVER

WITH: YOUR FAVOURITE PERSON IN THE WORLD

WHILE THERE: CREATE A ONE-MINUTE SCULPTURE IN A PUBLIC PLACE

TRAVEL TYPE: WINTER RETREAT

TRAVEL TO: THE UK

BY: PLANE

WEARING: INTERESTING HATS

CARRYING: A TRUNK

STAYING IN: A HUNTING LODGE

DINING ON: HIGH TEA

FOR: ONE WEEK

WITH: OLD FRIENDS

WHILE THERE: TAKE UP CURLING

TRAVEL TYPE: JUNGLE ADVENTURE

--- ✂ ---

TRAVEL TO: MALAYSIA

BY: DUGOUT CANOE

WEARING: BATTLE DRESS AND HIKING BOOTS

CARRYING: A SWISS ARMY KNIFE

STAYING IN: A HAMMOCK

DINING ON: TROPICAL FRUITS

FOR: ONE MONTH

WITH: A LOCAL GUIDE

WHILE THERE: PLAY RUBIK'S CUBE

TRAVEL TYPE:	**HONEYMOON**
TRAVEL TO:	**NIAGARA FALLS**
BY:	**GREYHOUND BUS**
WEARING:	**A TRACKSUIT**
CARRYING:	**A DISPOSABLE CAMERA**
STAYING IN:	**A RENTED MOBILE HOME**
DINING ON:	**FAST FOOD**
FOR:	**TWO DAYS**
WITH:	**HUSBAND OR WIFE**
WHILE THERE:	**WRITE POSTCARDS TO FRIENDS AND PARENTS**

TRAVEL TYPE:	**SPIRITUAL JOURNEY**

✂ -

TRAVEL TO:	**THE MIDDLE EAST**
BY:	**FOOT**
WEARING:	**A PILGRIM'S COSTUME**
CARRYING:	**A WISH**
STAYING IN:	**LOCAL HOMES**
DINING ON:	**THIN SOUP**
FOR:	**AS LONG AS IT TAKES**
WITH:	**YOUR SOUL**
WHILE THERE:	**LEARN THE LANGUAGE OF THE GODS**

TRAVEL TYPE:	**BACK TO NATURE**
TRAVEL TO:	**DESERT ISLAND**
BY:	**RAFT**
WEARING:	**NOTHING**
CARRYING:	**A GUIDE TO EDIBLE PLANTS**
STAYING IN:	**A HANDMADE HUT**
DINING ON:	**INSECTS**
FOR:	**UNTIL THE RESCUE TEAM ARRIVES**
WITH:	**A GUY CALLED FRIDAY**
WHILE THERE:	**TRY TO SURVIVE**

THE WORLD'S
YOUR OYSTER

The Age of Exploration was greatly consumed by the issue of mapping the world and recording it in great detail for the purposes of navigation and to indicate ownership. But others have seen maps somewhat differently.

In *Rodinsky's Room*[1] the Psychogeographic writer Iain Sinclair relates how a Jewish émigré named David Rodinsky retreated to his room above a London Synagogue before being committed to a mental asylum. Twenty years later, his room was rediscovered. Among his personal effects was his copy of the *London A–Z* street atlas, marked and extensively annotated in ink according to how Rodinsky thought the maps *should* be.

Maps also represent our cultural conception of the world. For example, they sometimes depict their country of origin in greater prominence than on those published elsewhere. One of the most famous depictions of emotional mapping is Saul Steinberg's map of the world 'as seen by New Yorkers', with Manhattan looming large and the rest of the world receding in the distance. Most recently, the *Atlas of Experience*[2] by Louise van Swaaij and Jean Klare from Holland published imaginary maps of emotional concepts such as 'Home' and 'Love'.

In the spirit of the Situationist Guy Debord, who liked to make cut-up maps of Paris, we invite readers to create a map of their own. The outlines of continents have been provided, but readers are free to colour, cut up and mark in borders – or not – as they so choose.

1. Rachel Lichtenstein and Iain Sinclair, *Rodinsky's Room* (London: Granta Books, 2000).
2. Louise van Swaaij and Jean Klare, *The Atlas of Experience* (London: Bloomsbury, 2000).

ACKNOWLEDGEMENTS

THANKS FROM THE AUTHORS

Rachael Antony: Rachael would like to offer her personal thanks to her friends who endured countless discussions about Experimental Travel and offered creative and helpful advice, and of course, to Laurence, without whom this book probably wouldn't exist.

Joël Henry: Merci à quelques secrétaires généraux, complices ou compagnons de route du Latourex :

Jean-Pierre Agasse, Bernard Aghina, Martine Amalvict, Michel Arnould, Robert Becker, Lydia Ben Ytzhak, Jean-Jacques Blaesius, Véronique Borg, Luc Bossi, Marie-Jo Brolly, François Burgard, Sylvie Braunstein,Yacine Canamas, Geneviève Charras, Pierre Chevallier, Guy Chouraqui, Chantal Convard, Marc Delorme, Joëlle Diderich, Michèle et Coco Diboune, Maria Dirks, Stella Duffy, Nelly Frossard, Véronique Ejnes, Alessandro Franzi, Theo Frey, Jocelyne Fritsch, Antonio Gasbarrone, Michel Gaschy, Gérard Gromer, Luc Gwiazdzinski, Manuel Halliez, Maïa Henry, Samuel Henry, Léo Henry, Line Henry, Michel Hentz, Bérengère Hill, Robin Huzinger, Corinne Ibram, Vladik Ivanenko, Bertrand Jérôme, Dominique Jung, Ursula Kauss, Claude Keiflin, Michel Krieger, Andy Kik, Sylvie Koullen, Christine Laemmel, Bernard Langlois, Jean-Pierre Le Goff, Hervé Lelardoux, Françoise Ligier-Fortin, John Livingstone, Christian Lutz, Denis Lutz, Wilson Martinez, Philippe Martz, Isabelle Mehl, Béatrice Meier, Bernard Meyer, Ariane Michaux, Hossein Mokry, Myriam Niss, Olivier Noble, Sylvie Pelletier, Ambroise Perrin, Jean Piero, Jean-Bernard Pouy, Hubert Prolongeau, Bernard Reumaux, Gustavo Rios, Jacques Rocchi, Nicolas Simonin, Nicola Smith, Kate Taunton, Jean-Paul Schweighaeuser, Jean-Charles Vernaelde, Robert Wagner, Messad Wagner, Hélène Weiss, Antoine Wicker, Giles Whittell.

CREDITS

This book was commissioned in Lonely Planet's Melbourne office by Laetitia Clapton, and its development was steered by Roz Hopkins. Production was managed by Bridget Blair, Jo Vraca and Andrew Weatherill. Daniel New designed the cover, and the book was designed and laid out by Daniel New, Radek Wojcik and Gerilyn Attebery. It was edited by Janet Austin and Adrienne Costanzo.

THANKS FROM THE PUBLISHER

This project could not have been completed without its many contributors, so a hearty thanks to our writer-travellers spread far and wide across the globe. Alex Landrigan translated the original Latourex experiments. Ben Butler interviewed Human Chess and the Degrees Confluence Project. The text of the Yellow Arrow experiment was provided by Christopher Allen and Jesse Shapins of Counts Media. At Lonely Planet Publications we'd like to thank: Thorn Tree Manager David McClymont for all his help in getting the project started; Leonie Mugavin and Liz Abbott, who helped with library requests; Lonely Planet staffers who provided amusing responses to a variety of odd spams; Laurence Billiet and David Collins at Lonely Planet Television, who developed a concept for a TV program about Experimental Travel, and whose research provided a strong starting point for this book; Karen Parker for her patience; Karina Dea, Jane Pennells and Jane Hart for design direction; Steve Caddy, Lara Cameron and James Hardy for layout assistance, Pepi Bluck for assistance with images; Fiona Siseman, Michael Tucak, Amy Carroll and Chaman Sidhu for legal advice. Our thanks also to the photographer Willy Puchner and his penguins; Stephen Hodge, of Wrights & Sites in Exeter; Michael Read for suggesting BYOA; Hamish Innes-Brown, Research Assistant at the Brain Sciences Institute, Swinburne University, for his brain-related assistance.

This book is also indebted to the numerous writers, artists and adventurers, both living and dead, whose ideas and spirit have informed this book. Unfortunately, for reasons of space, a number of writers' works could not be included in this book, so thanks to our unpublished contributors: Daniele Burzichelli (Sicily), Nelson Duarte (Lisbon), Cher Maxwell (Ontario), Laura Miller (Baltimore), Barbara Schlütter ('Zeller Land') and Ed Tahaney (New York).

**The following Experimental Travel games
were based on original Latourex experiments:**

A–Z Travel (Aléatourisme)
Aesthetic Travel (Esthétourisme)
Airport Tourism (Aérotourisme)
Alternating Travel (Tourisme Alternatif)
Anachronistic Adventure (Anachronotourisme)
Ariadne's Thread (Fil d'Ariane)
Blind Man's Buff Travel (Cécitourisme)
Budget Travel (Hypotourisme)
Bureaucratic Odyssey (Odyssée Administrative)
Counter Tourism (Contre-Tourisme)
Domestic Travel (Micro-Tourisme Aléatoire)
Ero Tourism (Érotourisme)
Expedition to K2 (Expédition au K2)
Exquisite Promenade (Promenade Exquise)
Literary Journey (Bibliodyssée)
Monopoly Travel (Monopolytourisme)
Nostalgia Trip version 2 (Tourisme-Fiction)
Opus Touristicus (Opus Touristicus)
Slight-Hitch Travel (Auto-Stop-Over)
Slow-Return Travel (Retourisme)
Thalasso Experimental (Thalasso Expérimentale)
Trip Poker (Trip-Poker)
Travel Pursuit (Filitourisme)
12 Travel (Dodécatourisme)

NOTES:

The Lonely Planet Guide to Experimental Travel

Published by Lonely Planet Publications

Head Office:
90 Maribyrnong Street, Footscray, Vic 3011, Australia
Locked Bag 1, Footscray, Vic 3011, Australia

Branches:
150 Linden Street, Oakland CA 94607, USA
72–82 Rosebery Avenue, Clerkenwell, London EC1R 4RW, UK

Published 2005

Printed by Printplus Limited, Hong Kong
Printed in China